PEOPLE, PROBLEMS AND GOD

BEGINNING PASTORAL COUNSELLING IN THE CHURCH

Peter Hicks

Illustrations by Dan Simmonds

Published by
The Baptist Union of Great Britain
November 1995

© Author 1995
ISBN 1 898077 12 6

Designed, typeset and produced for the Baptist Union of Great Britain by Gem Publishing Company, Brightwell, Wallingford, Oxfordshire.
Printed in Great Britain by Swindon Press Limited, Swindon.

CONTENTS

Preface

1. The material in this manual has been presented as a course of study. Study guides for individuals and groups are included after Unit 8; they should be consulted as each unit is studied.

2. Whilst those counselling and those being counselled can be either male or female, in the interests of political correctness we have tried to use he/him/his and she/her/hers in alternate Units, except where the sense of the text might be materially affected.

Author's Preface

If you've got one person in your church, you've got a problem.
If you've got fifty people, you've got fifty problems.
If you've got 500 people, you've got 500 problems.

So said a friend of mine as I was starting out as a new pastor.
Despite his cynicism, he wasn't far wrong. Christians are people
and people have problems – and maybe one each is a pretty
conservative estimate!

This course is about helping people with their problems, particularly in
the context of the local church. It is about pastoral counselling in the
widest and most general sense of that term. It is not a handbook for
pastoral counsellors in the more technical sense, and working through
the course will certainly not be sufficient to enable anyone to set
themselves up as a qualified pastoral counsellor; that requires full
training and nationally approved qualifications.

Even so, the need has never been greater for pastorally concerned
Christians with some basic knowledge of counselling skills and the types
of problems people in our churches are facing. In our house groups,
among our friends, in the church organisations we belong to, in the
wider family of the church, again and again we come across people who
may not be at the stage of going to a professional counsellor, but who
still need help. The fact you are interested in this course shows that you
are concerned for such people and want to become better equipped to
get alongside them and help them as far as you can. Working through
this course will do that for you.

Hopefully it will also do one other thing. Since you and I are just as
much people as those we seek to help, the course's insights into human
nature and problems will be relevant to us personally, will give us a
better understanding of ourselves and will help us to deal with our own
problems. If so, well and good. Indeed, I tend to feel that this would be
more than just a useful spin-off; it could be that the best basis for seeking
to understand and help others with their problems is that we are
walking with them along a path we have ourselves already walked.

Glossary

We will be using a number of technical and semi-technical terms in this study. Most of them will be explained when first introduced, but you may find the brief definitions below helpful.

anomie: loss of standards and fixed points, lawlessness.

behaviourism: an approach to understanding and helping people that stresses external experiences and behaviour and rejects the existence of an inner self such as the unconscious or the soul. See Unit 1.

biblical counselling: the approach to counselling developed by Larry Crabb. See Unit 2.

burnout: a condition arising from prolonged excessive stress, characterised by demoralisation, disengagement and hopelessness.

catharsis: dealing with the destructive power of experiences and emotions by bringing them to the surface and expressing and off-loading them, sometimes in dramatic ways.

clinical theology: the name given by Frank Lake to his Christian Freudianism. See Unit 2.

conditioned response: a term used by behaviourists for a response which would normally arise from a given stimulus when it arises from another stimulus that has been linked with the first (eg Pavlov's dogs salivating at the sound of a bell, when for them a bell was closely linked with the provision of food).

defence mechanism: a Freudian term for a subconscious device we adopt to cope with the undesirable desires that arise from the id.

directive/non-directive: approaches to counselling in which the counsellor controls the direction of the conversation/allows the person to control it.

eclecticism: selecting elements from the various approaches to counselling and joining them into a scheme.

ego: in Freudian terminology the conscious mind.

Freudianism: the approach to psychology and counselling initiated by Freud; psychoanalysis. See Unit 1.

Gestalt therapy: an approach to understanding and helping people based on concepts of the whole person and wholeness. See Unit 1.

id: in Freudian thought, the basic instincts and energies at the heart of the human psyche.

logotherapy: the approach to counselling advocated by Victor Frankl, stressing personhood and meaning. See Unit 1.

neurosis: a mental condition giving rise to anxiety, depression, obsession, and the like.

nouthetic counselling: an approach developed by Jay Adams, with particular stress on confrontation and directive counselling. See Unit 2.

presupposition: assumed foundational truth or principle.

paraclesis: encouragement, help, support.

projection: a defence mechanism in which a person locates in somebody else undesirable elements found in themselves.

primal pain: a destructive experience in early childhood or in the womb.

psyche: the inner self.

psychiatry: a medical term for the treatment of mental disorders.

psychoanalysis: the study and understanding of the person based on the analysis of the inner self; Freudianism. See Unit 1.

psychodynamic counselling: a development of psychoanalytic counselling which emphasizes the complex interactions in the person. See Unit 1.

psychology: the study of the human person, especially of mental process, emotions and the like.

psychotherapy: the applying of the insights of psychology to bring healing to the psyche, emotions, behaviour, and the like.

regression: a defence mechanism in which the person escapes from the unwelcome present by going back to behaviour appropriate to the past, especially childhood or infancy.

relativism: the rejection of fixed truth, standards etc, in favour of the belief that such things are relative to individuals.

repression: a defence mechanism, pushing unwelcome thoughts, experiences etc out of the conscious mind, and into the unconscious.

shalom: the biblical word for peace and wholeness.

superego: the Freudian term for the inbred conscience.

therapy: approach to healing.

trauma: an unpleasant experience which has far-reaching effects.

unconscious: the Freudian term for the part of the person where past experiences are stored without our awareness of them.

UNIT 1

SECULAR APPROACHES TO COUNSELLING

Like most things, pastoral counselling can be defined in a number of ways, some narrow and some wider. For our purpose we are going to use a fairly wide definition, since we want to be able to include things like listening, praying, and the ministry of the Holy Spirit as key parts of the counselling process, as well as talking and giving advice. Our working definition will be:

> **Pastoral counselling is a predominantly verbal and personal process of helping people in specific areas of need or concern. Christian pastoral counselling is pastoral counselling based on biblical principles and exercised under the direction of and in the power of the Holy Spirit.**

The demand for pastoral counselling in and through our churches is probably greater now than it has ever been. There are all sorts of reasons for this. They include:

- The breakdown of many of the structures of society – ethical, cultural, traditional, the family – leading to insecurity, hurts, and anomie.

- The rise of secular psychologies and therapies, proclaiming the message that if you have a problem you should see a counsellor.

- The teaching in some areas of the church that as Christians we have a right to expect that God (and so the church) will solve all our problems for us.

- The increasing number of people in our churches who have come from 'problem' backgrounds, including paganism, broken homes, traumatic experiences and involvement in the occult.

1

- The increasing rate, even in our churches, of things like marital breakdown and burnout.

- The policy of the state to use voluntary organisations including the church to do things formerly done by the health service or the social services, for example the care and support of people with learning disabilities.

At the same time, and largely in response to this demand, churches have been developing resources which particularly equip them to be involved in pastoral counselling, including:

- The development of small groups such as housegroups in which people are encouraged to be open about their needs and problems, and to give and receive help from others.

- The recognition of pastoral and counselling gifts in people other than ministers or pastors, and the setting apart of these people as elders, pastoral workers, housegroup leaders, and even pastoral counsellors.

- The ready availability of books, videos, and training courses on the subject of counselling.

- A new confidence in the Bible and the power of the Holy Spirit as effective resources in pastoral counselling.

EVERY CHURCH A COUNSELLING CENTRE?

How central is pastoral counselling to the ministry of the church? Does what we have just been saying mean that every church must develop a pastoral counselling programme as a part of its work and witness?

Some would say not. Counselling is now an accepted part of our secular culture. Psychologists, psychotherapists, works counsellors, careers advisors, Samaritans, Relate, etc are all providing an excellent service. If people have needs, let them use that service and let the churches get on with the things that are central to their life and which they alone can do, like worship, preaching, and evangelism.

Others would disagree. However good the secular counselling services may be, they would argue, they inevitably lack the one thing that for us is crucial – the distinctive Christian element provided by a biblical basis and

2

the presence of the Holy Spirit. Here is something that we alone can offer, and it is something that radically affects the whole counselling process.

My own position is something of a compromise. I accept that Christians have unique resources and that we should be using these wherever we can to provide counselling of a quality and effectiveness the secular agencies can never reach. But the fact is we cannot do everything. We are all confronted with needs, opportunities, and demands that far exceed our abilities to meet them. One of the biggest failings of most churches and many church leaders and workers is that we set ourselves too many things to do, and as a result do none of them well. However deeply I am committed to the importance of pastoral counselling, I readily admit there are plenty of situations where other aspects of church life will be much more to the fore, and it may well be right to take advantage of secular resources, simply because we have not the time or energy to provide a specifically Christian counselling ministry.

Having said that, there will be very few churches or church leaders who will be able to get by without supplying some specifically Christian counselling and, in addition, there will be some who will be conscious of God's call and leading to make this a significant part of their work and ministry. Where a church is able to supply a counselling service that includes all the resources of biblical understanding – the power of prayer and the work of the Holy Spirit, and the love and support of the Christian community, in addition to the insights that can be gained from secular counselling approaches – then it has something that is going to have a considerable effect, not just on the lives of the individuals counselled, but also on the other aspects of its life, including evangelism and worship.

WHO CAN DO PASTORAL COUNSELLING?

Everyone – particularly every Christian – can be involved in counselling. We all have the opportunity and the ability to support, encourage, listen and offer advice. We believe that the Spirit can use any of us in effective ministry to someone in need. Most Christians, of course, only get involved in counselling at a fairly basic level, since their knowledge and experience is limited. Some situations require expert counselling, and these are rightly left to those who qualify as experts. In God's way of seeing things, however, a decidedly non-expert listening ear and shoulder to cry on may be just as important as deep psychotherapy or specialist ministry.

3

We could separate out five levels of counselling, each of them vital in its own way.

1. **Specialist counselling**, requiring specific knowledge and experience in a given area, such as drug abuse. Here general counselling skills must be supplemented by special training.

2. **General professional counselling**, by someone who has been trained in counselling skills and understanding and who is able to offer help to all comers, though they would generally refer on any requiring specialist help.

3. **Semi-professional counselling**, by someone trained and qualified in, for example, Christian ministry or a caring profession, who has received instruction in counselling, and probably has had considerable experience. These too would be able to give at least initial help to all comers, but would generally have to work within severe restraints of time and availability.

4. **Non-professional counselling**, by someone not technically qualified, but aware of a gifting and calling which has been supplemented by reading and attending courses. Such counsellors would limit the range of people they seek to help, and would be very ready to refer someone on if they began to feel they were getting out of their depth.

5. **Everyday counselling**, in which we are all involved, as we seek to encourage and help and advise each other. No study of books is required for this; experience is a great teacher, and a reasonable level of sensitivity and common sense are essential to avoid making a mess of things.

This course is primarily designed for those at levels four and five – people who are already involved in some counselling, and who wish to develop further their understanding and skills.

COUNSELLING AND THE SPIRIT

You will have gathered already that I believe our counselling, if it is going to be truly Christian counselling, must be led and empowered by the Holy Spirit. This raises the question: if the Spirit is in charge, why bother to study counselling? Could we not simply say that he will give us the words to say, and do the work for us?

The answer is yes, there will be times when the Holy Spirit will take over in some special way, and we will be able to stand aside and watch him do the work for us. But that does not happen very often. As in preaching, or taking a children's group, the Spirit generally seems to choose to operate through our study and hard work, thus giving us the privilege of making a significant contribution to the process of helping the person. Of course we do our studying, and apply the results of our study, in conscious dependence on the Holy Spirit, always willing to let him correct us when we get it wrong. But we still have to do the study.

SECULAR COUNSELLING

In the rest of this unit we are going to look briefly at a few of the many secular understandings of counselling. For Christian counsellors none of them may be adequate in itself, though I believe they all have insights from which we can learn. As you work through them, you might ask these questions of each approach:

- What are the foundational presuppositions of this approach?

- To what extent do they fit in with the biblical understanding of people and their problems?

- What aspects of this approach appear incompatible with Christianity?

- What useful insights into human behaviour or pastoral care can we get from this approach and incorporate into our own approach to pastoral counselling?

PSYCHOANALYSIS

The most influential approach to counselling this century has undoubtedly been that of the psychoanalysis school, going back to Sigmund Freud (1856–1939) as its fountainhead, and developed by a wide range of Freud's followers, including Alfred Adler (1870-1937), Carl Jung (1875–1961) and Erich Fromm (1900–1980).

The term psychoanalysis, the analysing of the psyche or inner person, takes us to the heart of Freudian theory. We all have innumerable experiences, both pleasant and unpleasant, from the moment we are born, and even before. We consciously remember very few of these, but many of them are not completely lost. Deliberately or otherwise we let them sink out of our conscious memory into our 'unconscious', a part of us beyond the reach of the conscious mind, but where the experiences continue to live, and from where they can affect our feelings and behaviour. Though normally inaccessible, they do sometimes surface spontaneously in our dreams, and can be made to surface through things like hypnosis, the taking of certain drugs, or long term exploratory counselling.

All Freudian approaches to counselling are based on the belief that the unconscious part of us profoundly influences our personality and behaviour. Typically, a Freudian will reject immediate and 'obvious' explanations in favour of those which go deep into our unconscious. If a man, for example, decides to grow a beard, he might explain his action by saying he never has time to shave. The Freudian, however, would be sceptical of so simple an explanation, and would want to probe deep into such issues as "Why does he want to cover over his face?", "What is he trying to hide from?", "What causes his feelings of inferiority and inadequacy?" and "What experiences of rejection early in his life lie at the root of his behaviour?".

I remember a conversation I had with someone over breakfast about whether cornflakes should be eaten crisp before the milk soaks in, or left until they are soggy. She was a soggy cornflake eater and I was a crisp one. Moreover, I liked my toast cold and hard and she liked hers warm and soft. When it came to explaining our different tastes I was inclined to talk in terms of strong or weak teeth, or preference for silence at the breakfast table rather than the sound of steady crunching. But her Freudian approach rejected any such simplistic explanation. For her it all went back to infancy, feeding at the breast, and eating those mushy foods that came out of Gerber jars. Questions needed to be asked about my infancy: did I have a bad experience of breast feeding and baby foods? As for her, we needed to probe why she was regressing to infantile behaviour. Could it be that her childhood years (when she should have been enjoying boiled sweets and other teeth cracking experiences) were unhappy, causing her to pine for the security of mushy food?

Alongside the foundational insight of the role of the unconscious, Freud and his followers have developed many concepts which have had profound influence on our understanding of human nature and behaviour. One of these is the division of the person into three. Freud called the three parts the *ego*, the *id*, and the *superego*. The *ego* is the ordinary self we are conscious of as the experiencing subject. The *id* is a deep, mysterious and very powerful part of us, with strong, instinctive, basic desires and appetites, especially for self-preservation and sex. The *superego* is the part of us that learns that giving way to the desires of the id will very probably lead to disaster. It is a kind of conscience that monitors and seeks to control our behaviour. Inevitably, the id and superego are continually in conflict, with the poor ego stuck in the middle struggling to cope. A typical Freudian example would be a young child experiencing sexual desires (the id) which culture, particularly in the form of its parents, (the superego) forbid it from satisfying. So the child (the ego) feels frustrated or guilty and looks round to find ways of making the conflict more endurable.

To do this, the ego may develop certain techniques, or *defence mechanisms*. One of these could be *repression*. In order to cope with the desires coming from the id, the ego pushes them away, tells itself that they are not there, and behaves as though it has got rid of them. Sadly, say the Freudians, they don't go away that easily. They may be pushed out of the conscious mind, but the place they will be pushed into is the unconscious. There they will lie and fester, and sooner or later (often a long time later) push their way up into the person's life, perhaps in dreams, or in feelings and behaviour. Thus the sexually frustrated child may seek to cope by repressing its feelings and frustrations, and may do so satisfactorily for a time. The risk is high, however, that these repressed feelings will surface later in life, possibly giving rise to problems with sexual relationships as an adult.

A second defence mechanism is *regression*. This happens when the ego seeks to escape from an unpleasant present situation by recreating the experience of an earlier phase of life which was more pleasant. A child curling up into the foetal position or a thumb sucking teenager are popular examples, and many would fit the preference for soggy cornflakes in here too.

Another defence mechanism is *projection*. Instead of (or in addition to) getting rid of the unwanted feelings arising from the id by repression or regression, the ego may offload them by putting them on to others. If I find things in myself which my superego tells me are unacceptable, a good way of satisfying my superego is to claim that these things exist in someone else. If I focus hard enough on them in him or her, I can ignore them in me. My superego works overtime criticising and condemning them, and I am left in peace.

The Freudian approach to helping a person with a problem is based on the belief that his problem, which may take all sorts of shapes and forms, is the result of elements in the unconscious which probably go back many years, frequently to childhood, infancy, and even the womb. The aim of therapy is, therefore, to discover what these elements are, to analyse what experience or trauma caused them in the first place, and to dispose of them. This is no easy task, and it can take a great deal of time. Freud himself, for example, saw some of his patients several days a week for a number of years, and it is common today for a course of therapy to continue for over a year.

The counsellor will spend time building a relationship with the person, and developing a relaxed atmosphere in which he is able to open up. To help this Freudians have used drugs and various relaxation techniques. The person is encouraged to talk about himself and his past; the counsellor observes and listens, seeking to pick up clues, sometimes probing in potentially fruitful areas, always seeking to encourage repressed feelings and experiences to come to the surface. This, of course, can be a difficult and threatening process for the person as things he has sought to repress for years are being brought out into the open, and that can be very painful. Desires and emotions, as they surface, may be expressed in ways that are embarrassing, violent, or directed on to the counsellor; all this is to be accepted as part of the counselling process.

The counselling process is complete when the unconscious root of the person's problem has been discovered and brought to the surface, and expressed in such a way as to take away its power to continue to fester in the unconscious. This could be verbal expression in conversation, expression of emotion (tears, anger, screaming), or physical expression (violence, body movements).

A man, for example, might consult a Freudian counsellor for help over a problem of shyness. The counsellor discovers that when he was a child, his elder brother always did better than he did, and got most of the attention. The relationship between the two has always been good, and the man insists that he has never had any bad feeling towards his brother. As the counsellor probes further he begins to unearth evidence of resentment and jealousy. Under his guidance the man begins to express anger and hatred of his brother, and a desire to kill him, getting quite violent in some of the counselling sessions. The counsellor encourages him to do this, recognising that these feelings have long been repressed and have been the root of the man's inability to accept himself and so relate positively to other people.

PSYCHODYNAMIC COUNSELLING

Closely related to the psychoanalytic school is the psychodynamic approach to counselling, seen, for example, in the writings of Michael Jacobs. The substitution of 'dynamic' for 'analytic' highlights the stress that the psyche, or inner person, instead of being a static thing, and so able to be analysed, is dynamic and active. We are not an inert bundle of instincts and feelings but our inner person is alive with rich and complex relationships, both with people and things outside of itself, and, even more significantly, between the various parts of itself. Awareness of this dynamic functioning of the inner person is central to the counselling process. The counsellor's task, generally carried out in a non-directive way, is to enable it to be expressed and understood.

BEHAVIOURISM

Very different from the basic Freudian approach is that of the behaviourist school. Here the best known name is B F Skinner (b 1904); others are J B Watson (1878–1958) and Ivan Pavlov (1847–1936). H J Eysenck (b 1916) has advocated a modified form of behaviourism.

In strong contrast to the Freudians, the behaviourists make external behaviour and events the focus of their attention and the basis of their understanding of human kind. Rather than building elaborate – and unprovable – theories on some shadowy inner unconscious factor, we should follow a truly scientific approach, and study men and women just as a scientist studies any other object. Behaviourism can be summed up in a number of foundational tenets:

1. Human beings are animals and they function as other animals function. Indeed, we can learn a lot about humans by studying animal behaviour.

2. To understand them we need to study them scientifically, just as we examine any other animal scientifically.

3. The focus of scientific study is observed external behaviour. The scientist is concerned with the observable behaviour of water molecules at 100°C, not with their inner psyche.

4. Human behaviour is determined by external, not internal, factors. It is conditioned by the environment in which the person lives.

5. Certain factors, or stimuli, cause us to respond in certain ways. Most of these are natural and appropriate, but as we go through life we

tend to develop patterns of responses which are learnt patterns (conditioned responses) which are not necessarily appropriate or desirable.

6. Learnt responses can be unlearnt. Undesirable patterns of behaviour can be replaced by desirable ones by training the person to give the desired response to the given stimuli.

In seeking to help people, the behaviourist counsellor is not going to spend time looking for some shadowy inner factor buried deep within the person. His interest is in the person's behaviour. It is the behaviour that is the problem, and by dealing with the behaviour we find the solution. If our shy man were to consult a behaviourist counsellor, the focus of attention would be the man's present and future social relationships, not his family history. The counsellor might, for example, set the man a number of tasks over a period of time. Assuming, say, that he has found it impossible to inaugurate a conversation, his first task might be to say "Good morning" to the postman. When this has been successfully done, the next task could be to make a comment on the weather to the assistant in the paper shop. A third task could be to ask a colleague at work how she is. By modifying his behaviour by very easy stages, the man is beginning to move away from a pattern that is characterised by shyness to a more desirable one – until he ends up preaching on Speakers' Corner …

"I used to be shy and repressed until I discovered behaviourism. If it can do this for me, sisters and brothers, think of what it can do for you."

Though not as influential as the Freudian school, behaviourist principles have been accepted and followed by many, often with a reasonable level of success. Others have attempted in one way or another to combine the insights of the two schools.

CARL ROGERS

Carl Rogers (1902–1987) developed an approach to psychotherapy and counselling which has been very influential. Though influenced by

Freudian thinking, Rogers rejected both Freudianism and behaviourism as too deterministic. An American, he developed his approach in the United States in the second quarter of the twentieth century in a society that was strongly pragmatic, self-confident, and inspired by the American pioneering spirit and a strong belief in progress.

For Rogers, women and men are basically good. He specifically rejected the Christian teaching he had received as a boy that we are all inherently sinful. Each individual has within himself or herself what it takes to succeed, we do not have to continue with our failures and problems, for we have within us – in our real person – the resources to change for the better. The aim of counselling, then, is neither the Freudian one of unearthing the unconscious roots of our problems, nor the behaviourist one of the counsellor seeking to change our patterns of behaviour. Rather it is the actualising of the real person, enabling him or her to assert their true identity over the feelings, problems, or whatever.

The Rogerian counsellor therefore refuses to approach the person in need in any controlling or directing way. The key to progress lies in the person, so the counsellor's task is to create an accepting atmosphere in which the person can himself move towards self-realisation. Once a warm accepting relationship has been established, the person must be allowed to express fully all of his feelings. To enable this to happen the counsellor will adopt a very 'non-directive' approach, contributing nothing to the content of the conversation, but helping its progress by reflecting back to the person the things he says or the feelings he is expressing.

Our shy man, then, would be encouraged by a Rogerian counsellor to talk about his feelings and experiences: for example, how he reacts in the presence of a popular self-assured colleague, how he despises himself for his own inadequacy, or his experiences of social failure. The counsellor helps him give them full expression, and, to his surprise, so far from condemning him for them, almost seems to approve of them. Gradually he finds he is both understanding and accepting himself in a way he never did before. He begins to see that he does not need to be trapped in a pattern of failure and self pity, but he can move forward, accepting the person he is, and growing into the person he can become. With this new confidence he bids farewell to the counsellor, assured that from now on he is going to be the real person he can be.

As the counselling continues, the person finds it is possible in such an accepting and non-judgmental atmosphere to express and release emotions that have been formerly stifled, a process of catharsis. These may well be very negative emotions causing hostility, aggression and anxiety. The counsellor calmly accepts whatever comes, allowing the person free reign, in the belief that through this experience the person will gain self understanding and self acceptance, and, in due course, will gradually move from negative emotions to more positive ones.

GESTALT THERAPY

The Gestalt approach to therapy, particularly associated with the name of Frederick Perls (1893–1970), stresses the importance of working with the whole person. *Gestalt* is German for pattern or whole – a pattern of elements that make up a meaningful whole. If we are going to help people we must take account of the whole, body as well as mind, emotions as well as words. Every one of us, and every situation in which we find ourselves, is a complex whole made up of all sorts of elements in relationships with each other which are varied and developing. Hopefully we are able to experience these elements in their right relationships, in correct focus. Often, however, say the Gestalt practitioners, the wholeness is lost and our focus is wrong. We become fragmented, no longer integrated and the wrong parts dominate to the detriment of the whole.

The aim of therapy is thus to restore wholeness. The way it is done is wider than by counselling alone, which, as a verbal activity, is seen as failing to cater adequately for the whole person. The therapist will take a very active role initiating and facilitating experiments, exercises, bodily actions, role playing and open expression of emotion, often in a group situation. He is not interested in delving into the unconscious or the past. The focus is on the present and on the person becoming aware of who and what they are, how they function and behave, and what parts go to make up the whole. As awareness grows, the therapist helps the person to accept himself as he is, and to become willing to take responsibility for himself as he is. Only then can he begin to think in terms of development and change.

Our shy person, seeking help from a counsellor who uses the Gestalt approach, joined a small group that met fortnightly for a variety of activities, such as playing games and having meals together. To his surprise, he was not pressurised to join in the conversations, or to feel bad about his shyness. A basic principle of the group was that all were committed to accepting each other, and themselves, as they were. Gradually the activities and the open and accepting conversations helped him to grow in his understanding and acceptance of himself, and even to begin to talk positively about his shyness. As he watched others taking responsibility to change their attitudes and behaviour, he found that he was becoming willing to change himself. In the security of the group he experimented with role-playing, acting out self-confidence and assertiveness, and, backed with the group's ongoing encouragement and support, gradually put these things into practice in his wider relationships.

LOGOTHERAPY

Rogers' approach to counselling and Gestalt therapy are both basically humanistic, seeing women and men as essentially good and containing within themselves resources to solve their problems. In contrast, that of Victor Frankl (b 1905), a devout Jew who spent three years in various World War II concentration camps, recognises the importance of the spiritual element in human persons, and the existence of ultimate meaning which is rooted in God. Frankl's roots in existential philosophy (which stresses the priority of the human person over against, say, the scientist's approach which looks on human beings as machines) led him to criticise other approaches for their tendency to treat people as less than fully human. In contrast he sought through his therapy to enrich and stretch the individual as a person, stressing two areas in particular:

1. **Freedom and responsibility**. While the traditional Freudians tended to put the responsibility for our actions on the unconscious, and the behaviourists put it on our environment, Frankl insisted that though the unconscious and the environment do affect us very considerably, they do not control us. We are able to choose freely how to respond in any situation, and have a responsibility to respond positively, rising above circumstances and asserting the defiant power of the human spirit (as Frankl himself did in the concentration camps).

2. Meaning. The culture in which we live takes away meaning from us. Most of us operate within a narrow, often self-centred, concept of meaning, which needs to be stretched as we reach out to new ideas and people and ultimately to God. Meaning can and should be found in our attitudes, experiences and actions. In particular, suffering provides fertile soil for the development of our awareness of meaning. Confronted with pain, guilt and death, we can discover new attitudes and values, and thus become a more whole person.

Frankl's counselling method, known as logotherapy, does not follow a rigid pattern. More important than a structure is a responsive existential relationship with the person, and a creative openness to the way the conversation may develop. Some, but not too much, probing and analysis may be appropriate, but as soon as possible the counsellor will seek to turn the focus of the person's attention away from their needs and problems – the vacuum caused by their inability to see meaning in their lives – to the wide picture of life's significance, into which they are then able to fit the problematic pieces.

A shy man being counselled by a logotherapist found right from the start that his sense of significance as a person began to grow, as a result not just of what the counsellor said, but of the attitude and relationship between them. In time he came to realise that he had been letting what was in effect petty and minor fill his whole horizon. Why should all the potential of his unique God-given life be thwarted by the outside possibility that someone will laugh at him when he makes a suggestion? He still found it hard to rise above his shyness, but was greatly helped by the realisation that anything that is worthwhile is going to be costly.

UNIT 2
CHRISTIAN APPROACHES TO COUNSELLING

Welcome to Unit 2! Maybe as you ploughed your way through the various secular approaches outlined in Unit 1 you began to feel impatient. You began to wonder why we need to bother with all these non-Christian ideas and therapies; surely as Christians we simply need to get on with the Christian way of counselling. The secular approaches can be left to others, what we want is the true Christian way of doing it.

If that is how you feel, I'm sorry to say I have bad news for you. There seems to be no one true way of doing Christian counselling. Christians counsel in all sorts of ways, with almost as wide a range of approaches as the secular counsellors. There are those who evidently have accepted wholesale the insights of psychoanalysis or behaviourism, and follow them closely, incorporating a few Christian elements here and there. There are others who totally reject secular insights and attempt to develop an approach to counselling that is built purely on the teaching of the Bible. The snag there is that different people who have tried to do this have ended up with different systems. Then there are those who are selective in their use of secular ideas, sifting out those that seem incompatible with biblical principles, but retaining others and incorporating them into a general biblical framework. Even there the end products vary quite considerably.

The fact is that the Bible does not give us a clear blueprint for pastoral counselling, any more than it gives us a clear blueprint for the pattern of our Sunday worship. A moment's thought, of course, will give us reasons why this is a good thing. A pattern for counselling or worship that was right for the Jewish community in Jerusalem would probably not have been right for the church in Rome. What was right for the first century would not have been right for the fifth or fifteenth or twentieth centuries, and what is right for children would not apply to octogenarians. Given the variety of people and their needs, an approach that is right for one person may well be disastrous when tried on another. People vary, situations vary, cultures vary, problems vary, times vary, attitudes vary. There are so many variables that one fixed approach to counselling could never be sufficient to deal with them all.

What the Bible does offer is broad principles – parameters within which we can operate. The doctrine of God, his nature, his grace, and so on, is foundational, as is the biblical understanding of what it means to be human. In Unit 3 we will be looking at these and other foundational principles. Meanwhile I would suggest that, whatever other ideas and concepts a counselling approach may use, it must be faithful to these principles if it is to make a claim to being a truly Christian approach.

In this unit we are going to look at three approaches to counselling which do claim to be Christian. As we work through them you may like to assess them both in terms of their apparent relevance and usefulness in seeking to help people with problems, and in terms of their compatibility with your understanding of basic Christian principles and doctrines.

CLINICAL THEOLOGY - FRANK LAKE

We will start with Clinical Theology, an approach which has been heavily influenced by the ideas of Freud and his followers. Centred upon the thought and personality of its founder, Frank Lake, it has had wide influence in Britain, claiming to have trained over 15,000 people, most of them clergy, in 'human relations, pastoral care and counselling'.

Frank Lake (1914–1982) trained as a doctor and for some ten years was an Anglican medical missionary in India. He returned to this country in 1950, and took a post-graduate course in psychiatry. Aware of the need to train clergy and theology students in pastoral counselling, and with the backing of a number of Anglican bishops, in 1958 he started holding training seminars throughout the country. In 1962 he formed the Clinical Theology Association, run for many years from headquarters in Nottingham, and now based near Oxford. For some years Lake taught at the Anglican St John's College, Nottingham, and became quite involved in charismatic renewal, speaking at conferences on such subjects as inner healing.

In the mid 1950s Lake experimented with using LSD in treating patients with personality disorders. He discovered that, under the influence of the drug, what appeared to be the contents of the unconscious mind readily emerged into consciousness. In particular a number of his patients appeared to go through their birth experience again. On making enquiries of their mothers, Lake became convinced that they were accurately recalling what had happened. Building on this, he concluded that experiences from early infancy, birth, in the womb, and especially in the first three months of foetal development, were of vital importance in the formation of the person. Traumas and bad experiences then would shape the personality and emerge in later years in personality disorders. Thus, if we are to help people with problems later in life, the key to our approach must be to locate and deal with these 'primal' hurts. These could be, for example, the traumatic experience of the new-born baby who was separated from its mother immediately after birth 'kept waiting in a loneliness which becomes a panic, then a horror, and, beyond a certain limit, a dreadful splitting, a falling apart and fragmentation of the whole person, body, soul and spirit'[1]. But in his later years, Lake became convinced that most 'primal pain' was to be traced back to the early term of pregnancy.

1. Frank Lake. *Tight Corners in Pastoral Counselling* 1981 p 14

'Affliction in its worst forms strikes in the first three months after conception. It is not just the matter of whether the mother was pleased or not to discover that she was pregnant' (which can for the foetus be a 'shared delight at being wanted, or a horror at being a socially disastrous mishap'); all sorts of damage can be done 'before the mother even knows she is pregnant ... The foetus feels acutely the feelings which are the product of the mother's life situation, for better or worse, and her personal reactions to it . Before she knows that she is pregnant, the foetus knows what sort of a person this is, in whom he or she is fortunate or fated to be ... The evidence now available shows how severely the foetus can suffer at this early stage of its development. Most adults who have taken this retrospective journey recognise how closely the afflictions of later life, which had driven them to despair or near suicide, are faithful reproductions of crises first encountered in the earliest weeks of their foetal life. Before birth, the foetus may be seriously damaged if the mother is dependent on alcohol, nicotine or other drugs. It is also damaged by the less readily identifiable changes that transmit to the baby a mother's rejection of a particular pregnancy, and of the life growing within her. Any severe maternal distress, whatever its cause, imprints itself on the foetus.'

Frank Lake[2]

2. *ib* pp 15–16

Lake cites the vivid example of a number of American teenage girls who 'manifested an unaccountable tendency to break down suddenly into crying and sobbing'. On enquiry it was found that these girls had been in the early stages of foetal development when J F Kennedy was shot. Their mothers' reactions to the assassination were, suggests Lake, the cause of the girls' behaviour[3].

3. *ib* p 41

In seeking to repair the damage done by primal pain, the Christian counsellor's first task, says Lake, is to locate its source. This is no easy task; it is essential for the counsellor to develop a warm trusting relationship with the person, a non-judgmental 'therapeutic alliance'. This relationship is vital, not only to allow the person to relax and begin to open up to the counsellor, but as a crucial first stage of healing. In contrast to her primal experience of rejection and dereliction, the person is here experiencing acceptance and sustenance, primarily from the counsellor, but, because the counsellor is showing her the love of God, ultimately from God himself. Then, generally in a series of sessions over a long period of time, the counsellor gently probes into the person's past, adopting largely the role of listener, but unobtrusively directing the search in potentially fruitful directions. Again, for Lake, the counsellor is reflecting the attitude of God in Christ, who, besides speaking to us, is very much a listener, hearing and understanding us. The Holy Spirit, too, has a vital role in directing the counsellor in her approach, particularly at crucial moments. Though Lake started by using LSD in the counselling process, he soon replaced it with deep breathing techniques, or any general approach that enables the person to relax and allow the unconscious to surface.

"Well, you could be right. Grizelda was conceived just before Woodstock, and Nathaniel during a power strike."

Once the primal pain has been located, it is the task of the counsellor to help the person to face it and get rid of it. Again, this is done very much in an atmosphere of secure love and support. After years of running away from it, the person is gently helped to face and suffer the pain by expressing and reliving it, retracing her steps to the 'time and place of the original catastrophe or loss' and being led through it in a process of 'creative suffering'. Where, on the original occasion, 'the whole primitive person was split or fragmented', the adult is enabled to bear and assimilate the pain in a creative and healing way, and emerge whole.

Key to this is the cross. Lake focused in particular on two aspects of what happened at the cross. The first is that Christ's sufferings were that of an innocent person, and the second is that at the cross the anger of the world was vented on God. Christ's innocence parallels the innocence of the suffering foetus. The cross provides the place where the anger and hurt the adult has carried throughout her life can be off-loaded. God is able to take it, indeed he invites us to vent it on him.

Ultimately, says Lake, whatever is achieved has to be the work of the Holy Spirit. There comes a time in the counselling process when the counsellor has to stand to one side and let the Spirit do his creative and healing work.

Frank Lake's approach to counselling has a considerable following in this country, and can claim to have helped many people. For those Christians who are happy to accept its basic presuppositions, its strength is that, while many Freudian counsellors have little to say about what to do with the 'primal pain' or its equivalent once it has been located, Lake offers a specific – and Christian – solution. We don't just dig it out and leave it lying around, we deal with it in a positive way through the cross of Christ and the power of the Holy Spirit.

Nevertheless, in assessing the value of this approach, we could ask a number of questions:

- Is Lake's basic theory true? Though he claims there is much evidence for it, all the evidence is open to other possible explanations. In the very nature of the case, could it ever be shown to be true or false?

- Undoubtedly counsellors following the Clinical Theology approach have helped many people and are able to claim success for their method. Does success necessarily prove that their basic theory is correct? Could it not be that a lot of their results arise simply out of the experience of being loved and cared for in the long process of counselling?

- Do we always need to dig back to the root cause of people's problems before we can help them?

- Is this a truly Christian approach, or is it a secular (Freudian) approach with a Christian addition?

- Even if Lake's analysis is correct for some people, is it justifiable to try and fit everyone else into the pattern?

- Granted it is good for a Christian approach to draw attention to the cross, is Lake's use of the cross in counselling true to biblical teaching?

Very different from Lake's approach is that of the American pastor Jay Adams, who has written over thirty books outlining, sometimes quite aggressively, his theory of 'nouthetic counselling'. From a Calvinistic evangelical background, with a minimum of training in psychiatry, he rejects anything that savours of Freudianism in favour of what he claims is a wholly Bible-based system of counselling.

Adams' approach can be summed up in six strongly held principles.

1. Pastoral counselling is to be done by pastors, not psychiatrists. God has his own way of meeting the needs of men and women, and it is given in the Bible. Pastors who have the scriptures and the Holy Spirit have all they need. A psychiatrist without the Bible and the Spirit will inevitably fail to find the true answer to a person's problems.

2. Sin is the cause of all our problems. With the exception of organically caused behaviour (eg as the result of a brain tumour or senility), all problem situations arise directly as a result of sin in the person. Adams would not deny that my present problems may arise in part from some long past experience in which I was sinned against, but he resists very strongly that this means that I am not now responsible for my present behaviour. Childhood traumas may *affect* subsequent behaviour, but they do not *cause* it. A person who has, for example, been physically abused in their childhood, may well grow up with a propensity to violence, but she or he is still responsible for any violent actions – any such are still sinful. 'Sinful living is at the heart of the counselling focus'[4].

4. Jay Adams in G R Collins
Helping People Grow 1980
p 155

Questioned about, say, the man born blind in John 9, Adams readily accepts that 'problem' situations can occur without sin being immediately involved. The blind man wasn't guilty of sin, but nor, says Adams, was he in need of counselling. He was coping satisfactorily with his blindness. Had he responded to his blindness with anger or self-pity, he would have needed the help of a counsellor; but in that case, of course, he would also have been sinning.

3. The Bible is central to the counselling process. It is the counsellor's all-sufficient handbook. Granted, you do not go to the Bible to find out about car maintenance as the Bible makes no claim to provide such information. It does, however, claim to give God's answer to people's needs, and we are mistaken to look anywhere else for the answer. Long before Freud was ever thought of, the Bible provided principles and practices for counselling, and all that we will ever need to diagnose and treat people's needs. Adams cites 2 Timothy 3:16 in which the Bible provides the basis for four key steps in counselling:

a. teaching – outlining God's standards and requirements

b. convicting – bringing the person to conviction and confession of sin

c. correcting – leading the person into a new relationship with God and with others

d. training in righteousness – helping the person to develop alternative patterns of behaviour.

4. **Confrontation is central to counselling.** There are a number of words in the Bible which can refer to counselling. Adams concentrates on one in particular, the New Testament word *nouthesia/noutheteo*, which means 'to put in mind, to confront, warn, admonish'. Examples of its use are Acts 21:31 ('I never stopped *warning* each of you'), Colossians 1:28 ('We proclaim him, *admonishing* and teaching everyone'), and 2 Thessalonians 3:15 ('*warn* him as a brother'). This word contrasts with the much commoner word *paraclesis/parakaleo*, which literally means 'call alongside' and is translated 'encourage', 'exhort', 'comfort'.

The three elements of *nouthesia*, says Adams, are

a. concern: the counsellor sees a need and in love wants something to be done.

b. confrontation: presenting the person with the truth about God's standards, and their behaviour, and the need for action.

c. change: helping the person to move from wrong patterns of behaviour, wrong relationships, and so on, to biblical ones.

5. **Counselling leads immediately to action.** Adams does not see the need for a long series of counselling sessions. Once the person's sin has been located and the biblical answer outlined, the counsellor can go straight on to helping the person formulate a plan of action to put that answer into practice. This is to be done in a spirit of obedience to the commands and standards of God. We must not wait for our feelings or attitudes to change before we change our behaviour.

Rather, we change our behaviour so that it is in keeping with the Bible's teaching, and our changed behaviour will in due course change our feelings. The victory of Jesus Christ upon the cross, and the work of the Holy Spirit, are essential for this to happen, though Adams is careful to say that our obedience is needed too.

> Change occurs in Christians because Jesus Christ died for them, paying the penalty for their sin and freeing them from its power … Through Biblical direction by the Holy Spirit's power He enables us to recognise and overcome sinful patterns[5].

5. *ib* p 156

6. **Christian counselling is only for Christians.** The non-Christian will not only be unwilling to submit to the authority of the Bible; according to Adams, as a fallen sinner, she or he is unable to change to biblical patterns of behaviour. Thus, if a person is unwilling to become a Christian, the Christian counsellor cannot help them.

As Frank Lake, Jay Adams makes a number of good points in his approach to counselling, including his stress on the role of the Bible, and the importance of changing our behaviour even if our feelings have not changed. But, again, questions need to be asked as we seek to assess the truth of Adams' claim that nouthetic counselling is *the* way Christian counsellors should be following:

- Has Adams got his theology right? Is sin *always* at the heart of the counselling process?

- Is Adams really fair to the whole range of the Bible's approach to counselling? True, Jesus 'confronted' the woman at the well, but are there not times when the counsellor is called to 'weep with those who weep' rather than confront them with their sin?

- Can everyone's problems be dealt with by one or two counselling sessions and instructions on changing to biblical behaviour? Are there not some problems that are too deeply rooted to be dealt with in this way?

- Is it true that Christian counsellors cannot help non-Christians? Is there no common ground between us and them that enables us to do and say at least something that is beneficial?

- Could it be that nouthetic counselling is another example of an insight that is valid for some situations being pressed into service as the one and only answer to all our problems?

BIBLICAL COUNSELLING - LARRY CRABB

Our third example of a Christian approach to counselling is that of the American Larry Crabb. A trained clinical psychologist, he was in private practice for ten years, before leaving in 1981 to set up the Institute of Biblical Counselling to train Christians in what he saw as a specifically biblical understanding of counselling.

He claims to present a middle position between what he sees as two polarised extremes, represented for us by Lake and Adams. He accepts that 'people need to be deeply understood', but, equally, he accepts that, whatever the presenting problem, the root problem is sin 'in that people attempt to meet their needs through things other than God'. Similarly, on the issue of whether or not Christians should base their counselling on secular insights, he rejects both the wholesale acceptance of, say, the Freudian system, and its wholesale rejection. Instead, he says, we should start from a solidly biblical basis but be willing to build on it by incorporating all that is good in the secular systems, a process he calls *spoiling the Egyptians*.

The system that Crabb has built, following this process, can be summed up in nine propositions.

1. Human persons are made in the image of a personal God, with certain God-like capacities, notably to long, think, choose, and feel. But while God is infinite and self-sufficient, we are contingent and dependent on God. Problems arise when we seek to exercise these abilities independently of God.

2. Human problems are ultimately relationship problems: 'every non-organic problem is rooted in relating'. While the Bible may not deal directly with every type of problem, it has got the answer to the breakdown of relationships, with God, with others, and in ourselves. Counsellors 'need to build up biblical categories, add to them our observations from life, and reflect upon these prayerfully. In going through this process many times, we will gain understanding of what is going on'[6].

3. As persons we all have personal needs, central to which is the need to regard ourselves as worthwhile human beings. This need can be analysed into two parts: the need for significance, and the need for security. God has made 'the necessary and sufficient' provision for meeting these needs. Problems arise when we seek to meet these needs in ways other than through God.

6. Larry Crabb in 'Dr Larry Crabb' *The Christian Counsellor* 1.1 1991 p 8

'Carefully designed by God.'

7. Larry Crabb in G R Collins
Helping People Grow 1980
p 173

8. Larry Crabb in *Basic Principles of Biblical Counselling* 1975
pp 66–7

4. Significance is 'a purpose for living which will give me a real and lasting impact on my world and a purpose which I am completely adequate to accomplish'. True significance comes from the realisation that I am carefully designed by God, and from the surrendering of my life to follow his plan and live in the centre of his will. As I do this he gives me what I need to cope with each situation, and I am able to accept myself as perfectly designed and equipped for whatever God sets before me. Out of this comes the experience of fulfilment.

5. Security is 'the experience of being loved unconditionally by someone whole'[7]. All the security we ever need is to be found in God, who is omnipotent and sovereign. 'When the omnipotence and sovereignty of God are even feebly apprehended, I relax. God will meet my needs. No one can stop His love or the plans of His love. I am in His hands and there I rest secure'[8].

6. Problems arise when we seek to meet these basic needs elsewhere than in God. We start with a *wrong belief* about the way our needs can be met, believing, say, that our significance depends on what others think about us. The wrong belief leads us to set *wrong goals* as a means to meeting our needs, for example, the goal of being popular with everybody. Frequently we will fail to achieve our goals, landing us in anxiety, resentment and guilt, and even when we do achieve them we do not find them ultimately satisfying. Our problems escalate, and we find ourselves being enmeshed in *tangled webs*. The goal of being popular with everybody could lead us, for example, to anxiety ("What if somebody rejects me?"), fear (of doing something that will make me unpopular) or low self-image ("If others reject me I must reject myself"). We might even consult counsellors who tell us to change our behaviour patterns, or who trace our problems to a childhood trauma. But this, so far from helping, only complicates matters further, for our

root problem is not behaviour or past traumas, but a wrong belief about what gives us significance.

7. The counsellor's aim is to 'expose people to themselves' in a warm accepting atmosphere, so that they become aware of the wrong beliefs which are at the root of all their problems. The counsellor's approach will be directive, though not confrontational, using the biblical teaching to present the truth, and bringing the person to the point where she seeks forgiveness for her wrong beliefs and wrong behaviour, and starts afresh with a right relationship with the Lord, and so with others.

8. Crabb describes six steps in the counselling process:

   a. Identify negative feelings.

   b. Identify negative behaviour.

   c. Identify wrong thinking (which is causing the negative behaviour and feelings).

   d. Through teaching change the wrong thinking into right thinking. This, the 'renewing of the mind' (Rom 12:2), is the crucial step, and will include confession, repentance, and forgiveness.

   e. Plan right behaviour (which will arise out of right thinking – being 'transformed' by the renewing of the mind).

   f. Identify satisfying feelings, produced by right thinking and right behaviour.

9. Feelings must not be allowed to be the basis for behaviour. Even when we feel, say, insecure, we must base our actions on the truth of our security in the Lord, and not on our feelings.

Crabb's approach has a number of useful insights, such as the impossibility of finding ultimate fulfilment apart from God, the important role of our beliefs (right or wrong), our basic needs for significance and security, and the way we get trapped in 'tangled webs'. But, again, questions could be raised:

● Are the basic human needs for 'worthwhileness', significance, security, and fulfilment the right place to start building a biblical approach to counselling? Is Crabb not a bit too near Carl Rogers' humanism or the "I have a right to be happy" attitude for comfort? Should we not start with God and his character rather than ourselves and our needs?

- Is it always true that right beliefs will lead to right behaviour? What about the situation where a person knows what they should do, and wants to do it, but finds that they cannot do it, a situation perhaps described by Paul in Romans 7:19–20?

- Once again, this approach is for a Christian counsellor helping Christians; does it have anything to offer someone counselling a non-Christian?

SELWYN HUGHES

Founder of the Crusade for World Revival and the executive director of CWR's extensive training programme in Christian counselling, Selwyn Hughes is probably the best known figure in the field of Christian counselling for British evangelicals.

For some years he was a Pentecostal pastor, and he was influential in the early development of the charismatic movement in the UK. In his study of Christian counselling he has particularly benefited from courses he has attended in the USA. While generally eclectic in his approach, he is parallel in many ways with Larry Crabb.

We have come to the end of our brief survey of three very different contemporary Christian counselling systems. Perhaps you have warmed to one over against the other two and feel that that is the approach you would like to follow. Maybe you feel there are good points in each of them which you will be able to incorporate into your own understanding of Christian counselling, or perhaps you feel that all three of them are way off beam and we need to start from scratch to develop a truly Christian approach to counselling. Whatever our reactions, we each need to think through the principles, both biblical and practical, on which we are going to base our own approach to counselling, and it is this we will be attempting in the next unit.

UNIT 3
PRINCIPLES OF CHRISTIAN COUNSELLING

If we were asked to list half a dozen things that are central to
Christianity, we might well come up with the following:

God

Jesus

The Holy Spirit

Love

The Bible

The church

We will take these to give us six basic principles of Christian counselling.

As you work through these principles you may particularly like to:

1. Watch out for elements we touched on in our survey of some Christian counselling
   approaches in Unit 2.

2. Think through what these principles have to say about the extent to which we can use
   the insights of non-Christians into counselling that we were looking at in Unit 1.

---

1. Christian counselling is rooted in the nature and purposes of God.
If our counselling is to be called Christian, it must start with God.
Almost every aspect of the nature and purposes of God carries
significance for the way we seek to help other people.

The fact that God is sovereign *Creator* completely overthrows the
assumption that underlies so much of contemporary thinking – that the

universe (and each individual, as part of the universe) is the product of chance: I was not planned, I am an accident, what happens to me is random chance, it has no purpose. By contrast, as Christians we are convinced that the world and everything in it was planned and made by God and is upheld by him. Though sin and evil may do their best to destroy the beauty and goodness of God's creation and purposes, God is big enough to overrule them through his creative power and grace, bringing good out of evil, and 'working all things together for good' (Rom 8:28). Though it is certainly *not* appropriate to quote Romans 8:28 at someone who has just experienced a disaster, all our counselling can be undergirded with the confidence that God *is* in control, and, as we allow him, he will bring good one way or another out of even the most unlikely situation or experience.

'No man is an island.'

God's nature as *personal* highlights the importance of relationships. If, as we believe, God is a personal God, and he has made us as persons, able to relate to each other and to him, then the issue of helping people to relate rightly is going to be central to our counselling. The last few centuries have seen a tremendous stress in Western culture on the individual. Being an isolated individual is, however, not God's purpose for us (Gen 2:18). We are not complete on our own – we need others, and we need God. Wholeness comes from *shalom* in all our relationships.

Central to God's nature is *holiness*. Again, in contrast to the moral relativism of our culture, God is a God whose holiness throws into relief the difference between right and wrong, good and bad. In our counselling we have clear principles and standards by which to assess and direct behaviour and living. It isn't that God in some arbitrary way makes rules and standards for us to follow. Rather, we are to be holy purely and simply because he is holy. As people made in his image, we can only function truly as we function according to his holiness. Here we find parameters, a structure of right and wrong, good and bad, in which we can function and find security.

God's *love* not only sets the pattern for the counsellor (see below), it is also a great source of confidence and hope. Many of the people we seek to help will be in circumstances which appear to proclaim that life is meaningless or controlled by a savage deity. Others will be lonely, or feeling rejected by society because of who they are or what they have gone through. Others will be struggling with a low self-image, or self-rejection of one sort or another. Though it is hard for most people to grasp hold of, the knowledge that they are unconditionally and totally loved by the one Being in the universe whose opinion really matters, and who is the Lord of everything, is sufficient to enable them to cope with just about anything. Indeed, the potential is for something more than mere coping. Whatever the circumstances, says Paul (Rom 8:35–39) we can conquer, and be more than conquerors through his love.

An awareness of the *purposes* of God sets the goals we have in our counselling in their right context. We will doubtless have many short-term goals as we seek to help people with their needs and problems, such as supporting them through a crisis, helping them change an attitude, correcting an unsatisfactory relationship, alleviating their suffering or advising over a decision. All our short-term goals must be controlled by the declared purposes of God for each one of us. For me this is most clearly stated by Paul when he uses pictures about 'presenting everyone perfect in Christ', 'being transformed into his likeness with ever-increasing glory', and 'attaining to the whole measure of the fulness of Christ' (Col 1:28, 2 Cor 3:18, Eph 4:13). However far-fetched it may seem, God's goal for each person we are seeking to help, and so our goal, is nothing less than the very best that a human person can be, expressed in spiritual wholeness and Christlikeness. I personally believe that this is God's desire not just for those who profess to be Christians; he wants to see it happen in the lives of those who as yet have no faith in him or room for him in their lives. We are not limited in our Christian counselling to those who are Christians. We can, *as Christians*, counsel non-Christians, remaining faithful to our Christian principles, though very probably not parading them as such, and through what we are and what we offer, be part of God's great and often lengthy process of working in an individual's life.

SETBACKS TO SPRINGBOARDS

If we believe that God can work anything for good, and that his purpose is to present each person 'perfect in Christ', we can approach each counselling situation with the belief that, however great the problem or need, it can be an opportunity for growth and further unfolding of God's purpose for that person. We may not mention this to them, since in the pressure of the situation it may not be helpful. As we counsel them, however, we should be on the lookout for opportunities for growth: whether in understanding themselves, others, or God; or in character, as they learn and develop through the experience; or in their awareness of God and closeness to him; or in their ability to minister to others because of what they have gone through.

2. Christian counselling is at heart the ministering of Jesus Christ and his saving work to the person in need.

Perhaps the greatest thing about being a Christian counsellor is that it is not up to us to solve the person's problem. Granted, we will work hard to understand, and to apply all the wisdom and insights we may have. We do not however produce the answer – that is up to Christ. Whether it is forgiveness, or reconciliation, or peace, or self-acceptance, or healing, or strength, these things come not from us but from him. I like John Wesley's phrase by which he summed up his preaching: 'I offered them Christ'. True, he gave them doctrine, truth, advice and exhortation, and he told them about forgiveness and hope and peace and all the rest, but what he was basically doing was giving them Jesus Christ, the only one who could meet every need and situation.

In counselling, as in everything, Christ must have the supremacy (Col 1:18). Again, this will not necessarily mean that our counselling will be full of explicit references to Jesus, particularly if we are talking to non-Christians, but certainly it must be full of the truth of Jesus, rich with the love of Jesus, given in the Spirit of Jesus, and sharing the life of Jesus. If, as we believe, the cross of Jesus is God's answer to the fallenness and brokenness of the world, then the message of the cross must be key to all the counsel we offer. The message of the cross is so rich we can apply it in a number of different ways, as we have already seen when looking at the approach of Frank Lake. For me, two of the most significant aspects of the cross we can focus on in counselling are those of forgiveness and a new start, and the transformation of what seemed total disaster into something fantastic.

The salvation that Jesus gives covers the whole range of needs and hurts we will meet in our counselling – the finding of love and acceptance and self-worth; the healing of our brokenness, meaninglessness, rebellion, lostness, alienation, hurts and traumas; reconciliation, with God and with others; forgiveness, of our sins, of others, and self-forgiveness; cleansing; a new beginning; the conquering of death and sin and the powers of darkness; and hope for the future, both short-term and long-term.

Seeing ourselves as ministering Christ in our counselling takes a great weight off our shoulders – and puts a pretty heavy responsibility back on! The weight we lose is that of having to solve people's problems all on our own. The responsibility we get back is that of making sure we are people through whom Jesus can work. It is essential that a Christian counsellor should have a deep knowledge of Jesus and a close relationship with him. If he isn't a living reality in us, it is hardly likely his love and power and life will flow from us into others. Effective fruit-bearing is done by those who draw their life from the vine, and 'remain in him' (John 15:1–4).

WHAT EVERY COUNSELLOR SHOULD KNOW

Quite apart from a knowledge of counselling approaches, there are three vital things every Christian counsellor must know:

KNOW JESUS — A close walk with him and spiritual maturity are essential.

KNOW YOURSELF — A balanced understanding of yourself, your strengths and weaknesses, your prejudices and blind spots, your gifts and limits, will save you making many mistakes.

KNOW PEOPLE — Study people, their personality types, their temperaments, their attitudes and what makes them tick. Study the roles played by emotion, culture, background and tradition. Look at the effects of sin, of belonging to fallen humanity, of the powers of evil. Learn how to communicate, lead, encourage, motivate, inspire and make them feel appreciated.

3. Christian counselling must be led and empowered by the Holy Spirit.

One of the more unfortunate results of the current renewal of interest in spiritual gifts and ministries is a tendency in some circles to think of certain gifts and ministries as more 'spiritual' than others. Prophecy and healing, for example, are seen as very spiritual gifts requiring a high level of intervention by the Holy Spirit, while practising hospitality or playing the keyboard are 'natural' gifts which we can exercise more or less on our own. In particular, we might tend to think that there are two clearly distinct ways of ministering to people. One is through the exercise of spiritual gifts, through, for example, prayer ministry, words of knowledge, and the laying on of hands, an approach consciously very dependent on the leading and intervention of the Spirit. The other is through counselling, something we do with our 'natural' skills, without the need of any special attention from the Spirit.

I'm not happy with this division. The New Testament lists of gifts seem to make no such differentiation and, as I see it, Christian counselling should be as much a 'spiritual' activity as is the exercise of any of the more spectacular spiritual gifts. If our counselling is going to be truly Christian, it must be as much led and empowered by the Spirit as any other form of Christian ministry. It may generally be the case that the Spirit's leading or intervention in the counselling situation is rather less immediate and spectacular than might be expected in a prayer ministry situation. That does not mean it is any less real. The Spirit can direct us as surely through the exercise of our own mind and application of our own wisdom as through a word of knowledge. His power can flow into a person's life equally through the laying on of hands and through a lengthy series of counselling sessions.

For me the ideal is a merging of the 'prayer ministry' and the 'counselling' approaches. Our counselling should be done in conscious dependence on the Holy Spirit. Prayer should be foundational and whatever we say in our analysing, diagnosing and therapy should be Spirit led, whether through directly given insights or through our hard thinking. The help or healing given should be his work, even when it is mediated through our love and support and wisdom.

If, as you are counselling someone, you believe the Spirit is directing you to some specific area, or speaking in some special way, be careful how you pass this information on to the person. It may be very impressive to be able to say "The Lord has just told me your real problem is X"; but most of us are not very good at hearing clearly what the Lord is saying, so it may be wiser to be less direct: "I think the Lord might be saying something to me about X; does that mean anything to you?"

It is worth remembering that the name Jesus gave both to himself and to the Holy Spirit (John 14:16), the *paraclete*, means encourager, helper, supporter, comforter – an excellent definition of what counselling is all about. In the last analysis he is the counsellor, we are the people through whose gifts and wisdom and hard work he chooses to operate.

4. Love is foundational to Christian counselling.

There is much that can be said under this heading, but it can be summarised in the four following points:

a. Many of the people we will be counselling will be suffering from a lack of love – rejection, alienation, broken relationships, fear, low self-image and various emotional needs. Very possibly they may have met with rejection from some parts of the Christian community, especially if they have failed or sinned in some way. Their need for true Christian love will be great.

b. Value the person as a person, and never look on him as a 'case' or a 'client'. Seek to relate to him as Jesus would. Make sure that your motivation in counselling is pure. It should be for his good and not for your own ego boosting, voyeurism, feeling of power or source of gossip. If any of these things start surfacing, deal with them ruthlessly.

c. Accept them as they are. Watch your personal reactions and avoid any traces of reactions such as prejudice or rejection. Often it will be hard for them to come to you for help in the first place, so make it easy for them to open up to you. Spend time building a secure trusting relationship in which they feel relaxed. Whatever they confess to you, don't show shock or a judgmental attitude. Take what comes as it comes; you will have opportunity later, if necessary, to pass comment. When people are pouring out their problems and failings, don't say anything that will make it harder for them. If they express pent up emotions, tears, anger or frustration, let them do so. Do what you can to release them from any embarrassment they may feel, and, where necessary, learn to hide your own.

d. Give them your undivided attention. Listen to what they are saying and let them speak. They need to off-load, and you need to hear what they are saying. Very rarely interrupt. If it is not easy for them to off-load, encourage them with your obvious attention and concern, nods, encouraging comments, reflecting back in short phrases what they have said so that they can continue on the same track. Never make the mistake of thinking out your reply while they are still speaking to you, or pre-judging the issue before they have finished talking, keep listening! Most of us are far better at talking than at listening, so work hard at becoming a great listener. Listen not just to their words, but to their attitudes, emotions, the things left unsaid and their body language.

LOVE'S LIMITS

Love means that our self-giving and involvement with the person will be total while we are with them. But, since we have to operate within our human limitations, it is vitally important to bear three things in mind:

1. Train yourself to switch off from the emotions and pressures of the person when you are no longer with him. We cannot carry everyone's burdens all the time, too many counsellors end up as wrecks through trying. Commit him to the Lord in prayer, and trust the Lord to carry the burden. Find ways (reading, absorbing hobbies, etc) of redirecting your thinking after a hard day's counselling. If you find you are waking up in the small hours and can't get back to sleep for thinking of other people's problems, take it as a sign you need a break!

2. Avoid letting the person become too dependent or making excessive demands on you. Love calls for involvement and self- giving. But love equally requires that we help people take the right amount of responsibility for themselves, and we prevent them manipulating us or their situation in a way which will in the long term be damaging to them. Share the responsibility of caring for those with long term problems or major emotional needs with others, so that no one individual is overwhelmed.

3. Beware of any risk of sexual involvement. It is terrifying to hear of the number of counsellors who get sexually involved with the people they are trying to help. But the Devil knows his job, and the emotionally charged intimate atmosphere of the counselling room can be fertile breeding ground for trouble. As a general rule, only counsel someone of the same sex. If you have a spouse counsel as a couple. Even with same sex counselling, don't ignore the risks. Remember the godly minister who was accused by a teenage boy he was counselling of making sexual approaches. The man was almost certainly innocent, but enough mud was thrown in the local community to force him to resign his pastorate. If there is any element of risk, make sure you see the person in a room where you are not totally isolated. Have someone around who at any time might pop their head round the door to offer a cup of tea.

5. Christian counselling is based on the authority of the Bible.

Some approaches to counselling discourage directive input by the counsellor. For them the essence of counselling is listening, or enabling the person to find for themselves the answer to their need. Undoubtedly there are situations where such approaches are the right ones; but, equally, there would seem to be many where specific input from the counsellor is required, whether in the form of encouragement, advice, or instruction.

There are, of course, a number of different ways of appealing to the authority of the Bible, and it is up to us to select the one which is most appropriate to the person we are seeking to help. For a Christian who readily accepts the authority of each verse of the scriptures, it will be sufficient to read the appropriate passage.Others, Christians or non-Christians, may not be willing to accept such direct authority;though I have found that many people who might react against 'the Bible says' are prepared to listen to what is presented as 'the teaching of Jesus' or 'the Christian way of looking at things'. Sometimes, however, when no authority is acceptable, we have to do what we can, using, say, rational arguments to persuade the person to decide that what we accept on the authority of the Bible is in fact the most reasonable position to adopt or course to follow.

The Bible is a rich source of material for *instruction*, whether we are, for example, preparing a couple for marriage, helping an individual to cope with bereavement or sorting out broken relationships. Crabb's approach, built as it is on the counsellor's responsibility to help change wrong thinking into biblical thinking, is a good example of using the Bible as an authority for instruction.

A great deal of our counselling ministry will, I trust, consist of *encouraging and strengthening*. Here again the Bible has plenty of material to offer, with its rich teaching on such topics as the love of God, his grace and forgiveness and his promises. Even when people know these things in theory, there is great value in underlining them, and applying them specifically to their situation. We should not, for example, miss out on the value of pronouncing absolution. Many people find it hard to believe they are forgiven but, when they have confessed their sin, it can be a considerable strength and comfort to them to hear us clearly state (on the authority of the Bible and of God, not on our authority!) that their sins are forgiven. And, out of fashion though it may be, I still find value in giving people short passages of scripture to study and learn and repeat, in the belief that the promises and statements of God are 'living and active' (Heb 4:12) and have unique power to penetrate and change a person's thinking and living.

No-one can read Jay Adams without being aware that the Bible can also be our authority for *confronting* individuals with their sinful behaviour.

However we may react to Adams, there certainly are occasions when it is right to use the Bible to point out to those who claim to be following its teaching where they appear to be falling short. When we do feel it is right to do this, we need to take great care that our motives are pure, and, in particular, that there are no traces of anger or a judging spirit in us. We will have to work hard at building a positive relationship with the person, earning the right to speak what is on our hearts. We will also have to use all our wisdom and grace to avoid the person reacting negatively to what we say. There is something in human nature that wants to meet attack with attack – all too often a person will respond to being confronted by becoming angry, pointing out the faults in others or in the counsellor, or producing arguments why they are right. The danger of this reaction needs to be lessened by making sure the conversation is in a spirit of humility, love, acceptance and prayer. Finally, rather than giving the impression that we feel we have got everything right and he is wholly in the wrong, we need to approach the person with the attitude "Let's try and find out what God is saying to us in this situation".

6. The church is one of the greatest resources for Christian counselling.

Though there is great value in our contemporary pattern of counselling being done largely by specifically trained individuals on a one to one basis, I think we have something to learn from the way things appear to have happened in biblical times. There the community or the church as a whole shared the responsibility for caring for and counselling those in need. Everyone, not just the elders or leaders, encouraged one another and bore one another's burdens. We are each our brother's and sister's keeper, and in the community of the church we have a tremendous resource which the secular counsellor lacks and which we can use with great benefit.

The church community, even if it is small, will be rich in *experience*. Frequently there will be someone in the church who has walked much the same path as the person you are counselling. Though we must never type-cast or assume that one person's experience will be exactly the same as another's, there can be great value in encouraging those who have had similar experiences sensitively to get alongside and share, for example, how they adapted to retirement, came through depression or coped with a miscarriage.

Clearly, too, the church will be a rich source of *support*, ranging from practical help such as baking cakes and arranging lifts to hospital, through to "I don't understand what you are going through, but I am praying for you every day". Most churches have funds available to help those in need, and, again, people with skills and facilities that can be tapped. Two valuable resources in one church I pastored were friends with a large house in the country who were willing to take in someone for a couple of nights, and a travel agent who could fix up very cheap breaks in the sun at the drop of a hat.

The *teaching* programme of the church is another valuable resource. Ideally, many of the problems which people may need counselling for should be dealt with in the ongoing teaching and training ministry so that people are informed and equipped to face the problem issues before they arise. Many churches hold seminars and conferences on subjects such as marriage, bereavement and stress. Hundreds of Christian books are available on just about every conceivable subject.

Small groups such as house groups are another great resource for learning, support, experience, and for encouraging people to open up and share their problems and needs. Probably a small group like a house group should not be just pastoral in its purpose, since then it might run the risk of becoming excessively introspective; it needs to have other, more outgoing aims alongside that of caring for one another.

The church should also supply *support and supervision for the counsellor*. Counselling is costly, often draining us spiritually and emotionally. Those with a ministry of counselling should be recognised and prayed for publicly by the church, and supported by the prayers of the members. The counsellor should be supervised by an individual in the church, such as the minister, or by a small number of fellow elders, house group leaders, or the like. They will not only give advice about specific situations, but will keep an eye on the counsellor's own well-being, and step in if he begins to show any danger signals.

COUNSELLING AND MINISTRY TEAMS

Many churches are appointing and training teams of people for prayer ministry or counselling or both. Among other things this helps give such ministries a high profile in the church and makes it easier for people to ask for help. It also means that those engaged in these ministries are adequately equipped and supervised. Important for such teams are:

- An ongoing programme of training. We still have much to learn in these areas, both from each other, and from 'experts' we can invite in.

- Some standard of accreditation or recognition by the church. Not everyone who thinks they would like to do counselling is suitable for the task.

- Principles or guidelines for procedure. These will vary from church to church, but would include issues like opposite sex counselling and confidentiality.

- Mutual support. Helping one another, praying together, and bearing one another's burdens.

UNIT 4
ILLNESS, DEATH AND BEREAVEMENT

In the first three units we have been dealing with some of the issues involved in the theory and principles of counselling. For the rest of the course, we are going to look at specific areas in which we may find ourselves seeking to help people. These are: illness, death and bereavement, marriage and sexual issues, conflict, low self-image, and child abuse. Inevitably, this is a very selective list. It would take a course much longer than this one to cover all the possible issues any individual might meet in their counselling, but, hopefully, as we look at these areas, principles will emerge which can be usefully applied in other areas.

We start with a group of issues which are familiar to everybody: illness, death and bereavement. In our consideration of illness we will separate 'general' illness from terminal illness.

ILLNESS

Perhaps the two biggest issues in the pastoral care of those who are ill are the answer to the question "Why has this happened to me?", and the matter of prayer for healing. Before we look at these, I will highlight four things out of the many that could be said about ministering to those who are ill.

1. **Counter the dehumanizing effect of illness.** Illness, particularly if it involves a stay in hospital, tends to dehumanize us. We cease to be in charge of our own lives, and submit to doctors and medical staff who make us do things we would never choose to do. We stop being a person, and become a patient, or a case. Our family and friends suddenly start treating us differently, and talking about us behind our backs. All this is disturbing and threatening, quite apart from the pain and anxiety that generally accompany illness. The pastoral counsellor

"He's rather an unusual case…"

has a significant role in countering this dehumanization, by relating to the person, for example, in as normal a way as possible, by reassuring them, and reasserting their significance and value. A time of illness is a great opportunity for a person to discover how much they are loved, and how much they mean to so many people.

2. **If possible, help the person to view their illness positively.** Our culture tends to think of health as an automatic right, and illness as in every way undesirable and evil, something wholly negative and to be avoided at all costs. Whatever our theology of suffering, one of the greatest gifts we can give to those going through illness is the ability to look on their time of illness positively, an experience through which, for example, they grow as individuals, and learn new things about themselves, others and God.

3. **Allow the person to be honest.** When we are ill we go through a range of emotions; physical weakness may well mean we are less able than usual to cope with them. The pastoral counsellor needs to accept that there will be some times when it is right for the person who is ill to keep up a pretence – for example, a brave front when the children are around. There are other times when she will seek to give permission to the person to be honest, and to face up to and talk through her fears, anger, anxieties, and other such feelings.

4. **Minister the love and healing of Christ to the person.** It goes without saying that we should avoid anything that takes advantage of her weakness or embarrasses her in any way. Generally speaking, a person who is ill needs encouragement and love rather than counselling or deep theological instruction. Whatever our theology of

physical healing, Christ is the Healer, and we have the privilege and responsibility of ministering him. We do this largely through who we are, and our general conversation. We may well, in addition, choose a Bible passage to read which should be easy to follow with a straightforward and relevant message – often a single verse will be sufficient. We should ask her permission to say a prayer, and, again, keep it short and simple, praying for her, her family, and her immediate concerns. It may be suitable to hold her hand, or put a hand on her shoulder, while praying.

"WHY HAS THIS HAPPENED TO ME?"

Everybody asks this question at some time or another. Often it arises out of genuine bewilderment over how a God of love could allow us to suffer, but sometimes it is more a protest, an expression of anger, for which a merely intellectual response would be unsuitable and inadequate. Even where we do feel it is right to try and give some explanation in response to the question, we would be wise to start by acknowledging that we do not know the full answer; we have no quick formula that solves what is perhaps the deepest mystery of human life. But that does not mean there is no answer, even if it is only known to God.

Things we might choose sensitively to mention could be:

- Illness and suffering are an integral part of the broken world in which we live. Even as Christians we still share in what it means to be human, and to live in the world.

- There is a natural tendency to feel that suffering is a punishment from God for some wrong we have done, and, conversely, if we have been good, we shouldn't suffer. These ideas are contrary to the Christian message, which has the cross at its heart. We may choose briefly to point out, say, the examples of Job, and Paul in prison.

- Illness, despite all its negative aspects, can be a beneficial time in which we get things into a different perspective, slow down, take an enforced break, learn new things about ourselves and others, and so on.

- God too can use illness positively, to bring about things in our lives that could not otherwise have happened. The cross demonstrates that God is big enough, wise enough, and loving enough to bring ultimate good out of any situation.

PRAYER FOR HEALING

Like so much in this course, my comments on this topic will reflect my own thinking and practice. I presume we are all learners in this area, and your understanding and approach to prayer for healing may be very different from mine; but, hopefully, some of these comments may be helpful.

1. **Approach.** Styles of praying for healing vary greatly, from casting out the sickness in the name of Jesus, to a gentle 'if it be your will' approach. I suggest we select our style according to where we are at, but also with an eye on the person we are praying for and her understanding and expectations. We may favour anointing with oil, as a sign of the presence of the Holy Spirit, or the laying on of hands; we may pray one-to-one, or call in a small prayer ministry team, or suggest that the church leaders be invited to minister (James 5:14). Prayer can take place in the context of congregational worship, special 'healing' services, communion services, house groups, or in private.

2. **Discerning God's will.** On occasion we may feel that God is telling us that the person will be healed, or, possibly, that they will not be healed. My own feeling is that great care should be exercised in how we pass on this information. We don't always get 'words from the Lord' right, and much damage can be done when we get them wrong. Perhaps the most we should allow ourselves to say is "I believe that the Lord might be telling me that you are going to healed". Similarly, I would normally include something parallel to "Nevertheless, not our will, but yours", either in my praying, or when I am talking about the prayer with the person.

3. **Authority**. Acknowledging that God may not necessarily answer the prayer in the way we want does not prevent us praying specifically and with authority. Some choose to express authority by raising their voice or speaking directly to the illness. I would generally stress the lordship of Christ, and the authority that is ours as children of God, or God-appointed leaders in the local church, to pray in his name, and in obedience to his specific command to heal those who are ill. Though we may not have a carte blanche promise that all we pray for will be healed, we have a right to pray for healing, and should exercise that right with confidence and expectancy.

4. **Love**. We should of course respect the wishes of the person in the matter of prayer for healing. Some may have reservations about the nature of prayer, or about God's intervention in our lives; an older person may have reached the stage where they are looking forward to dying. The choice about prayer for healing must be hers. However strong our theology of healing, or our desire to see signs and wonders, our only motivation must be love for the person.

5. **Explanation**. Where necessary and possible, prayer for healing should be preceded by explanation of what we are doing, why we are, for example, anointing with oil or laying on hands, and what might (or might not) happen as a result. In particular, we should help equip the person to cope if it should happen that healing does not come at once, or in the way we have asked.

TERMINAL ILLNESS

A great deal of study has been done on the way people react to death, both to the knowledge that they or a loved one is about to die, and to bereavement. It has been observed that there are common elements in most people's reactions, though it needs to be emphasized that every person will react differently, and that there is no fixed pattern that each must go through. The reaction to terminal illness will be experienced not just by the person who is ill, but also by family members and close friends. A knowledge of what is to be expected can help the counsellor, and can be very useful in helping the people involved to understand and cope with their reactions.

1. **Denial**. Our bodies and minds are so made that our first reaction to any personal disaster is to deny it: "This can't be happening to me". Such a denial is in effect an unconscious defence mechanism as the news is too awful for us to take on board all at once; it would destroy us. We are therefore cushioned. At first we reject it, warding it off through denial, and only gradually let it sink in. The counsellor will accept the value of a comparatively brief period of denial, but should watch in case  it goes on for a long time. The person, for instance, might refuse to accept he diagnosis and irrationally insist on a second and third opinion, or there might be an unhealthy insistence that God must

heal her. In such cases it may be right to seek to help the person face up to reality.

2. **Anger**. Denial is a way of rejecting the awfulness of imminent death. So too is anger. We reject the prospect of death by being hostile to it. But since hostility to the prospect of death is not easy to express, it often comes out in other ways – anger at medical staff for not diagnosing the cancer sooner, anger at God for allowing it to happen to us, or simply anger vented on those nearest to us for no apparent reason at all. Such expressions of anger can be very disturbing for the person and her family, especially if they are out of character. The counsellor will need to explain that this is a 'normal' reaction, and to help the person and her relatives to off-load their anger in ways which are helpful rather than destructive.

3. **Fighting**. Another expression of rejection is a fighting spirit: "I'm not going to let this thing beat me". It can also be expressed as a bargaining attitude, possibly with God: "If I become a Christian, will you give me back my life?", or with the illness itself: "If I can just live until Christmas, then you can have me". Again, the counsellor will seek to channel this kind of spirit in positive rather than counter-productive ways.

4. **Despair**. As the person works through the various stages of rejection, she begins to emerge into the first stage of acceptance: it is real, it is happening to her, there is no escape, she is going to die. Often this stage brings depression and a feeling of hopelessness – the 'cords of death entangle and overwhelm them' (Ps 18:4–5). Here, far from rebuking the person for lack of faith, or whatever, the counsellor will need to show great love and compassion as she walks with her through the dark valley.

5. **Acceptance**. In time, hopefully, the person will begin to emerge from the darkness of despair, and adapt to the the knowledge that she is soon to die. This can give her a period almost of peace, which can be a beautiful time, when she 'sets her house in order', and spends precious time with her loved ones.

Talking about death

Our cultural norms make it hard for us to talk about death, even when we are Christians, and our Christian cultural norms tend to make it hard to talk about the darker side of the process of dying. Again, the counsellor must avoid forcing the issue, and must be very sensitive as to where the person is at in the process of rejection and acceptance. But hopefully there will be occasions when it will be right to raise the subject and talk through how the person is feeling about death, her questions and fears, and the like. A balance has to be kept between the darkness of the suffering and separation involved, and the hope that is ours through Christ's victory over 'death on the cross. Again, we will have to admit that we do not have all the answers, but just talking about the issues, expressing fears and uncertainties, and being ministered to in love and prayer, can be of tremendous value. As previously, the reading of carefully chosen passages of scripture can be helpful; passages I have used with Christians are Philippians 1:20–24 (with some explanation) and Isaiah 43:1–3a. Most people, whether they are Christians or not, will let you read Psalm 23 to them.

Death and the non-Christian

Richard Baxter, in *The Reformed Pastor*[1], stated that while he had reservations about death-bed conversions, they were always worth trying! In these days we are very conscious that we must avoid anything that smacks of taking advantage of or browbeating the dying person, yet most of us would love to share something of the Lord with her as she sets out on the journey to eternity. Again, sensitivity and love are vital here. We must not force the conversation into a direction she does not wish. I have found that most people who are dying are willing to let you say a prayer for them, perhaps after reading the twenty-third Psalm. When praying such a prayer I have sought to express it in such a way that they can readily understand it and make it their own, and in so doing can 'call upon the name of the Lord' and put themselves into his gracious hands.

1. Richard Baxter 'Visiting the Sick' *The Reformed Pastor* s 2.4.4.7 in the original edition, pp 102–4 in the Banner of Truth edition, ed W Brown 1974

Helping a Christian through death

A generation ago the general attitude towards death was that it was something to be resisted right up to the end. The growth of the hospice movement, and new thinking about death and dying, have made it easier to 'die with dignity', and to get a little nearer to the (probably idealized) picture of the saints of old who called their family to gather around them, imparted good advice and blessing to all and sundry, and then chose to 'depart in peace'. I have often been called to the bedside of a Christian, with the knowledge that there is only a very brief time to go.

Even if she does not appear to be conscious, there is a possibility that she can still hear what is being said, so I always assume she can. I generally make a practice of holding her hand while praying with her, and have had the shock at the end of the prayer of a squeeze of the hand from someone who was supposed to be in a coma. Lengthy ministry at this stage is rarely called for. Rather, a simple acceptance that this is the end of life on earth, that God is going to take her through the experience of death into his eternal life, prayer for strength and grace particularly for those who are being left behind, and a final committal to the love and mercy of God.

BEREAVEMENT

The loss of a loved one is possibly the most shattering of all human experiences. As in most areas of pastoral care and counselling, there are no easy formulae telling us what to do and say. Much of our ministry will be our expression of love, 'weeping with those who weep', being a rock when everything else is giving way.

'Stages of grief'

Grieving is a process which generally lasts for two to five years. Some would suggest that though the grief grows less acute, it never goes away totally. People have discerned various stages in the grief process. Again, these are not fixed or inevitable; in my experience they tend to merge into each other, and many people will move from one stage to the next, then slip back to an earlier one.

1. **Shock**. As we saw above, we react to something as terrible as bereavement with initial denial and unbelief. For the first few days a bereaved person is likely to be in a state of emotional numbness, often unable to distinguish reality from fantasy, and functioning to a large extent on auto-pilot.

2. **Emotional release.** Tragically, our British culture has tended to inhibit the full expression of grief, in contrast, say, to biblical times, when it was quite acceptable to tear your clothes and weep aloud. Most agree that expression of grief, generally through tears, is a valuable part of the grieving process, and it should not be discouraged.

3. **Anger and guilt**. As we saw above with terminal illness, hostility towards the awfulness of bereavement can often be expressed as

anger or resentment at others, at doctors, at God, or at themselves, where it may come out as guilt ("Why wasn't I a better wife/husband?" "Why didn't I do more to avoid their death?").

4. **Yearning.** For a year and more, most bereaved people experience disorientation, listlessness, apathy, restlessness, loneliness, sadness, despair, irritability, and depression.

5. **Illness**. Quite often a bereaved person will go through a bout of illness, which, though genuine enough, is actually part of the body's reaction to the shock of loss.

6. **Acceptance and reorientation**. Gradually, with many ups and downs, the person grows in her acceptance of her loss and acclimatizes to life without her loved one.

Immediate bereavement counselling

The need for 'counselling' in its more technical sense in the early days of bereavement will probably be small. The bereaved person may well ask "Why has God allowed this to happen?", but almost certainly this will not be the time for careful explanations; she is unlikely to be able to take them in, even if we attempt to give them. What is needed in the early days of shock and numbness is compassion, love, companionship, practical help – the giving of ourselves rather than the giving of our wisdom. Who you are and what you do is much more important than what you say; a hug and shared tears will convey far more than a carefully thought out speech.

The counsellor will want to make herself readily available during the early days of bereavement, and will also make it as easy as possible for the bereaved person to express her feelings, and, in particular, to express her grief. It is quite likely that the person (if 'British' and Christian) will feel that it is somehow weak or wrong to mourn. The counsellor may need to explain that weeping is a natural and helpful way of expressing grief, grief itself is an expression of love, and if we did not love her, we would not grieve at losing her; but we do love her, and our tears express that love.

There is a bewildering mass of things to be done in the days immediately following a death. Help can be offered, though most of the technical matters will need to be dealt with by the next of kin or the executor. In my experience undertakers, bank managers, and the like are very helpful at these times. In addition, the DHSS publishes a useful booklet *What to do after a Death* (D49).

The funeral

The significance of the funeral in the process of bereavement and grieving can be very great. The elements of looking back and thanksgiving for the life of the person help set the death in its context; the coming together of family and friends, and the sharing of memories of past experiences during the get-together after the service, all contribute towards this. The funeral is also a decisive break in which we say farewell to the body, and know that we will never see it again – the reality of the loss is vividly presented. For those who have not yet been able to weep, the funeral can be the catalyst for emotional release. However much we may want to make a Christian funeral a triumphant occasion, it is vital that this element should not be excluded and we should make it quite clear to those who have been bereaved that it is perfectly acceptable for them to express their sorrow as well as their confidence in the ultimate victory of Christ. Hopefully, too, the funeral service, the prayers, the things said, the ministry of Christ, the love and sympathy of those who are present, and the message of death conquered and life eternal, will all be a rich source of comfort.

Mourning

The process of grieving takes years rather than weeks. Interest in and support for the bereaved person generally begin to drop off after the first few weeks. The counsellor will need to continue to be available, and to help her work through her emotions and experiences, however long that may take. Points to bear in mind during this normal grieving process are:

- The bereaved person will experience many mood swings; she may cope well for a time and feel she is 'getting over it', and then, for no obvious reason, be plunged into depression, anger, or the like. The counsellor needs to be able to accept these swings, and to help the person through them, reassuring her that this is all part of the process of grieving.

- Talking about the person who has died should be encouraged; though the person has gone, memories are there to be treasured. There need be no rush to dispose of clothing and so on – wait until the bereaved person feels ready to do it. Unless it is unavoidable, major changes like moving house should not be made shortly after a bereavement as maintaining elements of continuity with the past can help to make the loss more bearable.

- Elements of unreality and fantasy, quite understandable in the early days, may continue for some time, and should be handled gently and compassionately. Vivid dreams, "I heard his voice saying my name", "I had this tremendous feeling that she was there with me in the room", are ways in which the brain reverts to what has been so familiar in the past, and the person should be helped to understand what is happening.

- Anger may surface in any number of ways and the counsellor should seek to help the bereaved person understand where it comes from and to off-load it. It may be possible to channel the anger in a positive direction; at the time of writing, for example, parents of children killed in a tragic minibus crash are campaigning vigorously to make minibus seat belts a legal requirement.

- Feelings of guilt and regret should not be dismissed; they may be ill-founded, but they are nevertheless real. The counsellor will encourage the person to talk and think them through, remembering the positive as well as the negative, and then take them to God in prayer for grace and healing.

- Though readily available, the counsellor will not always be alongside the bereaved person during the long process of disorientation and gradual reorientation. As time goes by she needs to be helped to develop her own resources, ways of coping with her feelings, people she can contact when she is lonely, new interests that will fill the gap, and so on.

- Watch for anniversaries, or other events that may trigger an emotional reaction.

Problems in the grief process

No grieving is easy, but things become particularly difficult when the process somehow goes wrong. The bereaved person fails to move through to eventual acceptance and reorientation, and somehow gets stuck at one of the stages on the way. This can be caused by several factors. There may be some problem in the person herself, or in her relationship with the one who has died. There may be special circumstances in the death such as suicide or sudden death, or the bereaved person may have been at least partly responsible for it, as in a car crash. The failure to grieve normally in the early days, through cultural or misplaced Christian pressure, can also lead to complications later on.

A person may, for example, get stuck in the earliest stages of the process, and find it impossible to accept that her loved one is dead. Clothes and her room in the house are kept just as they always were, ready for when she walks through the door. Another person will be unable to distinguish fantasy from reality, being convinced, for example, that she is receiving messages from her loved one. Anger can become excessive, or guilt or depression can be prolonged indefinitely.

The counsellor's task here is to recognize that a problem is arising in the grieving process, and to seek to understand what is causing it. This may not be immediately obvious – prayer, discernment, and a lot of time spent with the person may be needed before it comes to light. Once the cause of a problem in the grief process has been understood, it can hopefully be dealt with, and the process allowed to continue. Simply treating the symptoms will not be effective.

John's wife, Mary, died of MS in her mid-thirties, after a long illness, leaving him to care for the two children. At first John appeared to be coping well, sorting out Mary's affairs, and adapting the family routine; he seemed almost relieved that the long process of suffering was over. After a few weeks, however, Mike, the church pastoral worker, noticed that John was becoming increasingly withdrawn, was beginning to neglect the children, and was spending long periods daily at the graveside. At first Mike thought that John's behaviour could be understood in the light of the long hours he had spent caring for Mary during her illness. As he encouraged John to talk with him about his feelings, and his relationship with Mary, it began to emerge that all through her illness John had been carrying a growing anger and resentment at Mary for ceasing to be the wife he wanted her to be, and in effect through her illness and her death deserting him and leaving him the responsibility of the children. For the most part he had kept this anger under control, but now that she was dead, he had turned it in on himself, and was consumed with shame and guilt that he should have felt this way towards his wife in her time of need. The times spent at the grave were a desperate search for atonement and forgiveness.

Mike's first task was to allow John to express his feelings as fully as he could, taking great care not to condemn or criticise him. Then he sought to help John understand the source of his anger in that it was not basically an anger against Mary, but against the MS. Though John inevitably bore the responsibility for his actions, his feelings were not something abnormal, but something most people in his situation would experience. Building on this, Mike helped John gradually to move to the point where he could begin to forgive himself, and to seek and receive forgiveness from God, and, in a sense, from Mary. At the same time he tried to redirect John's energy which up to now had been wholly consumed in anger and guilt, into more constructive channels, particularly in building a new life for the children. It was a slow process, with many setbacks, but John gradually learnt how to cope with his emotions; visits to the grave became less frequent, and he was able to continue in the more normal process of grieving.

UNIT 5
MARRIAGE AND SEX

MARRIAGE PREPARATION

On a number of occasions I have carried out a poll of married Christians to find out how much marriage preparation they were given before a church wedding. The result has always been alarming. Frequently over one third had no preparation at all, and the majority of the rest just one or two sessions. People who had been given years of training for their careers spent less than a couple of hours being specifically prepared for the most significant of all human relationships.

Some aspects of marriage preparation are best done by the person who will be conducting the wedding. That does not mean to say they have to do it all. A good arrangement is for a number of couples in a church to be trained in marriage preparation. A couple preparing for marriage can then be allocated to a specific couple, who will not only be responsible (under the oversight of the minister or person taking the wedding) for the preparation, but will also hopefully continue indefinitely after the wedding as friends and advisors.

The number of sessions required will vary greatly. Some engaged couples will have read widely and discussed all the issues together. In an ideal church there will have been ample teaching through the youth group and house groups and from the pulpit on the principles and practices of Christian marriage. Sadly, however, some couples are unbelievably naive, and have never got round to thinking about many of the issues, let alone talking them through together. In an age when the majority of our young Christian couples were not themselves brought up in Christian homes, it is generally unwise to assume that they have any real idea of what Christian marriage is.

Sue and Richard are Christians and plan to get married in six months' time. The minister agrees to take the wedding, and explains that it is the practice of the church to require all couples to go through a process of marriage preparation. Jack and Pat, a middle-aged couple who have been trained as part of the church marriage preparation team, agree to be responsible for this.

Jack and Pat see themselves as having three main responsibilities:

1. To develop a relationship of friendship and trust with Sue and Richard, so that both couples can be open with each other in the months up to the wedding, and keep in close touch with each other after the wedding.

2. To help Sue and Richard face and think and talk through at least some of the issues, and thus give them experience and models for dealing with other issues that will arise.

3. To teach Sue and Richard about Christian marriage, both from the Bible, from their own experience, and from the experience of others. They are wise enough to realise that they must avoid any elements of paternalism here. Rather, the approach must be "Let's look at Ephesians 5 together and see what it really does say about Christian marriage", or "This is a problem we had to face, or a mistake we made – you may be able to learn something from it".

With the first point in mind, they have Sue and Richard round for meals, share social activities together and talk freely and honestly about themselves.

To help Sue and Richard face up to issues, they use the technique of getting them separately to write down answers to questions, reading them aloud, and then the four of them together responding to the answers and talking them through. The kind of questions they use are:

- What are my strengths? What are my weak points?

- What are my fiance(e)'s strengths/weak points?

- What is marriage?

- How does Christian marriage differ from ordinary marriage?

- What is love, and what is distinctive about Christian love?

- What do I think the role of the wife should be in our marriage?

- What do I think the role of the husband should be?

- How should our commitment to Christ be reflected in our marriage?

- What should we do when we disagree?

- Given that all marriages are under pressure, what do we think might be the special pressure points on our marriage, and how do we think we might deal with them when they come?

Jack and Pat soon find they have material here for many hours of discussion. For example, Sue's list of Richard's weaknesses, and Richard's reaction to it, could alone provide enough for half a dozen sessions. They are aware, however, that not every issue has to be sorted out here and now. The most significant thing is that Sue and Richard are learning to talk creatively through matters that will be crucial to the success of their marriage.

In fact so much time is taken on these issues that Jack and Pat's third area of responsibility, of providing teaching, looks like being pushed out. But this is not too worrying, as a good deal of teaching is going on in the discussions, including referring to relevant Bible passages. Jack and Pat also have a favourite technique which they use to good effect with all the couples they prepare for marriage: they get Sue and Richard to read Dave and Joyce Ames' book *Looking up the Aisle* to each other, each reading aloud a section at a time, and then discussing between the two of them the issues raised. When they have gone through that, there are several other books they will recommend, including Janet and John Houghton's *A Touch of Love*, specifically covering sexual aspects of marriage.

The minister will see Sue and Richard for two or three sessions. In the first he explains the various aspects of the service, and goes carefully through the traditional vows, explaining what they mean, and underlining the commitment involved in words like *forsaking all other* and *for better, for worse*. He makes a practice of encouraging couples to rewrite the vows so that the words they use will be very much their own choice. Similarly he gives them wide choice in the form the service takes, so that it will be as significant and personal as possible to them. In a final session, just days before the wedding, he goes through the practicalities of the service with them.

WORK AT IT

The myth lingers on that successful marriages just happen, without any real input from the individuals concerned: 'As long as they love each other, everything will be all right'. At the risk of sounding morbid, the counsellor will need to stress that successful marriages never just happen. Indeed, all the pressures are in the other direction: a marriage that is left to itself will wither and die. Marriages have to be worked at, just as a career has to be worked at to make it succeed. Each partner needs to be continually working at a growing and developing relationship, richer love, and deeper understanding. Tendencies to get into a rut, get bored with each other, take each other for granted, become selfish, and so on, need to be actively resisted.

MARRIAGE COUNSELLING

There are two types of marriage counselling – the first we see far too little of, and the need for the second is far too great.

Counselling for couples who do not have problems in their marriages may at one time have seemed unnecessary. But now few doubt the value of *marriage enrichment* and the like. Many churches are holding special weekends, and giving couples opportunities for taking stock and rededicating their marriages, perhaps at significant anniversaries. In an ideal world it might be the accepted norm that, with the help of a trained counsellor, all couples would periodically take stock of their marriage, just as individuals take part in appraisal exercises in their secular jobs.

Almost all marriage counselling which is taking place is seeking to help a marriage in trouble. In my experience any Christian counsellor who is experienced and capable in this area will be overwhelmed by requests for help. In the secular sphere our local Relate branch currently has a five month waiting list.

At the risk of seeming to oversimplify what is a very complex task, here are ten pieces of advice for those who are embarking on this type of counselling.

1. **Get in early.** It is far easier to deal with problems while they are still small than when they have developed to the point where the couple are talking about divorce. Granted, it is not easy for a counsellor to approach a couple about apparent problems in their marriage, though

this may sometimes have to be done, even at the risk of a rebuff. The suggestions two or three paragraphs back might make early trouble shooting more possible.

2. **Get each partner in the marriage to commit themselves to finding the solution to their problems.** In my experience counselling in a situation where one partner is not prepared to make any effort to save the marriage is hopeless. They must both be committed to do everything they can, even if only for a limited period. "We'll give it three months, and really try to make it work in that time ."

3. **Build a relationship of trust and confidence.** Marriage counselling can be threatening to the couple as it involves revealing very personal weaknesses, and admitting to serious failures. Little progress will be made if the individuals remain defensive, and are not willing to be open about their faults. Further, counselling may well need to be pretty directive, giving specific steps the couple need to take to make progress. All this means that it is very important that the couple have confidence in the counsellor.

4. **Look for causes, not just symptoms.** Symptoms are generally easy to find: "He spends every evening at the pub"; "She never wants sex"; and so on. The hard task is to get behind the symptoms to the root causes, since these will rarely be obvious even to the individuals. Why every evening at the pub? "Because that's where my friends are". But is that the real reason? Why does he need to get out of the house? Why does he no longer want to spend evenings with her? Does she nag him about jobs round the house? Is he bored with her? Is going out a subconscious way of 'getting at' her because she has done something he resents? And if, say, this last suggestion is true, why does he react to what she has done in this way; why does he sulk and manipulate instead of facing the issue and talking it out with her?

5. **Establish ground rules for discussion.** Frequently, problems develop in marriages because the couple fail to communicate adequately. The counsellor needs to help them to do this, both in order to make progress in the counselling sessions, and, hopefully, as a model for future communication in the marriage. A counsellor might require the couple to follow a pattern something like this: The counsellor asks A a question; B must not interrupt while A is answering;

when A has finished, B must state in his own words what A has been saying (to ensure that he has been listening adequately); only then may B give his own version of the answer to the question, again with no interruption from A; then A gives her summary of what B has said.

6. **Take feelings seriously.** A lot of the issues that are brought up will be factual: "She's always round at her mother's", "He never helps with the children". Though discussion of facts can sometimes be a basis for progress, they are often very difficult to establish: "Of course I help with the children; I play football with Tim". Feelings, on the other hand, are incontravertable. She feels he doesn't love her like he used to; whether he does or he doesn't (and that is pretty hard to establish!) there is no denying that she feels that he doesn't. The counsellor will take that feeling seriously, helping the husband to be aware of it, and accept its reality, and, hopefully, helping them both to work out ways of dealing with it.

7. **Base the counselling on God**. Even when counselling non-Christians, it may be possible to pray with the couple, and make it clear that you are basing your counselling on Christian principles. This particularly applies if the couple were married in church, starting their marriage with at least some place for God. Where the couple are Christians, not only should the counsellor emphasize basic Christian principles like faithfulness to vows, forgiveness, and Christian love, but, through prayer and ministry, the love and grace and power of God should be invited in to heal and restore and strengthen. As we have already seen, this kind of ministry does not replace the sessions of counselling and the commitment to hard work on the part of the couple, but it is an essential part of truly Christian counselling.

8. **Help the couple to decide on one or two specific areas for action.** Marriage problems are often very complex, and it can be helpful to isolate specific issues the couple can begin to work on. If progress is made in these, it will hopefully give them encouragement to tackle other issues in due course.

9. **Wherever possible, get the individual or the couple to decide what specific action is to be taken.** If she feels he doesn't love her like he used to, try getting each of them to suggest things he or she might do to counteract this feeling, and then to select what seems the most helpful – with the commitment to go away and do it, and come back next time to report on what has happened.

10. **Make use of all resources available.** If the couple are willing, you may be able to tap into the experience and expertise of others in the church, for example, people who have been through similar crises, those with financial know-how, or a doctor. I have found it useful to know of places where I could send one or both partners away for a few days' break, possibly with financial help from the church 'communion fund' or its equivalent. This could be just a breathing space, or somewhere like Green Pastures in Bournemouth will also have experienced counsellors available. A 'Marriage Enrichment' or 'Marriage Encounter' week-end may be suitable, though it needs to be stressed that these week-ends are designed to make good marriages better, not to restore shattered ones. And, of course, there are always books which can be recommended. If you are getting out of your depth, you will need to know of other counsellors to whom, with their permission, you can refer the couple.

LOVING IS GIVING

A lot of love is strawberries-and-cream love. I love strawberries and cream because of the pleasure I get from them, not for the pleasure I can give to them. There's nothing wrong in this; I could argue that strawberries and cream were created to give me pleasure.

But in the relationship between wife and husband love that remains at that level is inadequate and sub-Christian. My wife was not created solely to give me pleasures. She was also created so that I could enrich her and give her joy, even if doing that is costly and difficult for me. Christian (*agape*) love doesn't love for what it can get out of the other person. The Good Samaritan didn't get a kick out of helping the wounded Jew; it was doubtless the last thing he wanted to do. But he did it – and, says Jesus, that is love. In my counselling I often need to stress that love is something much more than the pleasure I feel when my wife does something that gives me a kick. Love is doing something for someone else, for my wife, which does little or nothing for me, but something for them. Love may often include getting, but its richest heart is giving.

COUNSELLING PEOPLE WITH SEXUAL PROBLEMS

There are two opposite reasons why people may not seek help for a sexual problem. In the current climate they may not view something like lust or homosexuality as a problem. Or, for many Christians at any rate, they may be afraid to admit that they have a problem, since to do so would be to confess failure as a Christian. Here the right combination in the counsellor of clear Christian principles and an attitude of non-condemning acceptance is more important than ever.

Anyone who gets involved in counselling in this area needs to be very aware that they are putting themselves at risk. They too are sexual beings and there are inherent dangers in talking with another person about sexual matters. The counsellor needs to keep a very close check on his motives and reactions, lest, say, elements of voyeurism or unhealthy interest begin to appear. Tragically, far too many counsellors who have set out to solve someone else's sexual problems have ended up having sex with them. Here, more than anywhere, the counsellor needs to observe the principles of not counselling someone of the opposite sex, and, where appropriate, of counselling in pairs. Don't stroke the serpent, kill it!

Probably very few married couples escape having sexual problems at one time or another. Many go for years without satisfying intercourse. Most go through patches when intercourse is not possible, or is hard for one or the other. During such times there may be intense sexual frustration, possibly giving rise to unfaithfulness. It is probably true that all sorts of pressures and problems in a marriage can be coped with if the sexual side is satisfactory – you can have a blazing row, and then make up and make love, and all is well. If the sex life is dead, there is that much less to hold the marriage together when problems arise.

Confronted with a situation where intercourse has ceased, the counsellor will need to help the couple decide whether the cause is primarily physical or psychological. This may not be as easy as it sounds, in that physical symptoms like frigidity or impotence can arise from psychological factors. If it seems fairly clear that there are no major psychological causes, then the couple should be referred to a doctor who will pass them on to a specialist. The success rate of treatment in this area is usually high.

Psychological causes could be of two main sorts. The individual may be consciously or unconsciously withholding intercourse because there is a problem between him and his partner, or it may be that there is a problem from another source which is being transferred or projected on to the relationship with his partner. In the first case, for example, a person may be carrying deeply ingrained anger or resentment at his partner. In the second, a person may have been sexually abused, giving him, say, a fear of intercourse . In this kind of circumstance, the counsellor might adopt a combination of Freudian and Behaviourist approaches, seeking to help the couple analyse and understand the root causes of their problem, and then dealing with the anger, or the results of the abuse, or whatever the problem may be, and at the same time helping them to find ways of expressing their love physically, short of full intercourse, but, hopefully, working towards it over a period of time.

Where there has been unfaithfulness in a marriage the counsellor will need to:

- Help the unfaithful partner to come to a position of true repentance, full renunciation of the relationship, receiving forgiveness from God and from the wronged partner, and forgiving himself.

- Help the unfaithful partner in dealing with the factors which gave rise to the adultery. These may vary from a passing weakness to a serious lust problem, or it may, as we have been seeing, be linked with sexual frustration within marriage. It would be wise to assume that a person who has fallen once in this area is especially at risk, so help may well be needed in how to face and resist future temptation.

- Help the other partner to cope with the sense of betrayal and the shattering of their relationship, and to come to a point of true forgiveness and acceptance.

- Minister the grace and healing power of Jesus Christ into the pain and hurt of the situation, through love, prayer, and the power of the Holy Spirit.

- Help provide an opportunity for a fresh start, possibly in the form of a rededication of the marriage in a service. A public act of recommitment of this sort can be very significant, though, of course, if the fact of the adultery is not generally known there is no need to announce that this is the reason for the rededication.

The principles and standards of Christianity are so opposed to the attitudes and practices of our sex-intoxicated society that it is not at all surprising that many Christians have major sexual problems, struggling with temptations and practices in the areas of lust, homosexuality, sex outside of marriage, compulsive masturbation, and maybe exhibitionism, child abuse, and transvestism. We will be looking at one of these, child abuse, in some detail in Unit 8. Here are some general principles for counselling in this area.

1. **Watch yourself.** Again, the counsellor will need to keep a careful watch on himself in the two areas of personal reaction and temptation. Confronted with someone confessing sexual sin, I need to be very careful that my own attitude does not affect the way I respond. It is hard enough for him to admit his weakness and failure; in no way must I make it harder by showing shock, a judgmental attitude or rejection. Our pattern here is Jesus and the woman taken in adultery (John 8:11). Secondly, however secure I may feel against being led astray myself, I need to take note of 1 Corinthians 10:12 'If you think you are standing firm, be careful that you don't fall!'. Better counsellors than me have fallen, therefore I must make absolutely sure I don't follow them.

2. **Have a clear understanding of biblical teaching on sex.** Many Christians are confused, torn between our present culture's attitude to sex that sees everything as OK as long as you enjoy it, and the idea that Christianity teaches that everything sexual is dirty. The truth is, of course, that the Bible teaches that sexuality, with all its attendant feelings, is pure and beautiful. Sexual attraction and pleasure are gifts from God, not in themselves dirty in any way. They only become sinful when they are used wrongly, when we pervert their use into forms of self-centred indulgence God has not authorised. Sexual sin is looked on seriously in the Bible, but it is not the greatest of all sins, nor is it in any way unforgivable. Sexual temptation is not sin, although consciously and deliberately letting the mind play with lust and fantasy certainly is (Matt 5:28). Probably the majority of Christians today would hold that homosexual feelings in themselves are not sin, and that the silence of the Bible on masturbation means that we should not be dogmatic on the issue. Homosexuality, however, moves over into sin when it gives rise to physical practices or specific fantasies, and masturbation which is accompanied by fantasies or where the person has lost control over his body certainly seems sinful.

3. **Try to find the cause of the person's sexual problem.** We do not need to know the source of the fire to put it out, and in many cases it may be that only a very experienced counsellor will be able to analyse why the person has his problem. It could be that there is a fairly obvious

cause of the problem which the counsellor can locate, and it can be of great help to someone who feels overwhelmed by the power of something he cannot control or understand to find an explanation of what is happening to him. Understanding where the problem comes from can be a vital step towards getting rid of it. Common sources of sexual problems are being sexually abused as a child, having an unsatisfactory relationship with the same-sex parent (meaning, for instance, that a boy identifies with his mother rather than his father, and tends to follow female rather than male sexual orientation), being a 'wrong-sex' child (where the parents hoped for a child of the opposite sex, and bring the child up accordingly), the need to assert sexuality when it is called in question by peers and the like (a non-macho young man needs to demonstrate his masculinity by his sexual exploits), or the longing to be accepted and loved (a person who has experienced rejection finds that promiscuity is a way of being noticed and in some sense loved).

4. **Sensitively assert their responsibility for their actions.** To balance up the teaching that I have a sexual problem now because of what others did to me as a child, I need to recognise that I am still responsible for my present actions. I do not have to let my past experiences control me. Plenty of people have had the same childhood experiences as me and have not let them control their sexual behaviour. Additionally, as a Christian, I don't have to fall into sin, however great the pressure (Rom 6:12–14, 1 Cor 10:13). The counsellor will need to be sensitive to the individual person in this matter, since some will be already so weighed down with guilt that it will be unhelpful to add to it. On the other hand a recognition of my responsibility for my action is not only an essential prerequisite for repentance and forgiveness, it can also give me hope in that I do have a choice – I can choose to act differently in the future.

5. **Minister the grace and healing of God into the person's life.** When issues have surfaced and the person is ready to seek forgiveness and healing, bring the whole thing to the Lord in prayer, confession, forgiveness of people involved in childhood situations and the like, specifically rejecting the sinful pattern of behaviour, and asking for the power of the Holy Spirit to set the person free from their bondage. It may be suitable, if the person is willing, to involve others, such as the minister and elders, in this. Though there will very likely be lapses in the future, and the person will have to renew this step, it can mark a decisive rejection of the pattern of thinking and action the person has

been following, and doing it before two or three witnesses can in itself be an added strength.

DELIVERANCE MINISTRY

An increasing number of Christians feel that sexual sin, especially where there seem to be elements of an external power taking control of the person and causing them to do evil, may well be specifically demonic in its origin, and thus that our ministry to such people should include deliverance. I personally am not at all sure about the concept of a Christian being demon-possessed, but I do accept that in one way or another the powers of darkness can get a foothold in our minds, and it may be that one of the commonest forms this takes is seemingly uncontrollable lust. I would always be slow to conclude that a person needs deliverance ministry, but feel that there is a place when ministering to a person who has been overwhelmed by sexual temptation in getting them to state the old baptismal vow of 'renouncing the Devil and all his works'. If I felt it necessary to go further than this, I would get together two or three church leaders and use the authority of Christ that he has given to us to declare the lordship of Christ over the person, and to rebuke any powers of darkness that are seeking to control her or him, telling them to depart. Any such ministry needs to be done with the full co-operation of the person, and followed by specific prayer for the infilling of the Holy Spirit.

---

6. **Help the person to develop new thought and behaviour patterns.**
   There will be all sorts of areas of the person's thinking that will need to be renewed, ranging from wrong beliefs and attitudes ingrained in him since childhood to the concept that other people's bodies are a legitimate object for his selfish sexual gratification, whether mental or physical. In the course of conversation the counsellor will help him measure up his beliefs and attitudes with the biblical teaching and with the mind of Christ. Out of renewed thinking will come new behaviour. It may be possible to discover a particular behaviour pattern which the person has been following. For instance, he falls when he is feeling depressed, or has suffered some sort of rejection. In this case the counsellor will need to help him think of other rather more positive ways of responding to feelings of depression or rejection. It must be accepted that deeply ingrained patterns of thinking and behaviour are unlikely to disappear overnight, but, through the power of the Holy Spirit, and with the determination of the person, change is possible. The counsellor will need patiently to encourage, even when there are lapses and progress is very slow.

UNIT 6
CONFLICT

Even in churches we don't have to go very far to find conflict, whether between individuals, or between groups who differ in background or outlook or aims. In this unit our main interest will be what to do when confronted with a conflict situation, but we will first spend some time looking at causes of conflict. This gives us the opportunity to do a bit more thinking about some of the reasons why people behave as they do, a subject we were only able to glance at briefly in Unit 3.

It shouldn't surprise us that conflict situations arise in our churches. After all, even an average sized church will contain people of a considerable range of background, cultures, ages and experience. No church is made up solely of spiritually mature and Christlike people; there will be some who are not yet Christians, young Christians, Christians who've never matured, and those who are on the way but still haven't reached perfection. Then there will be those who are under a lot of pressure at home or at work , or who are deeply affected by traumas and hang-ups from the past, or who are emotionally unable to cope, or who are full of conflict inside themselves. A pretty explosive mix!

Nor need we look on conflict as entirely a bad thing. Many of the things that accompany it are undoubtedly bad – fear, anger, self-centredness and division – but two people having two different views on an issue, or doing something in two different ways can in fact be a means of bringing about good. Rightly handled, the two conflicting approaches can be a source of learning and enrichment and progress. This is a theme we will pick up on later in this unit.

The New Testament has several examples of conflict: the disciples arguing over who is the greatest (Luke 22:24), the dispute over food distribution to widows (Acts 6:1–7), the events leading to the Council of Jerusalem (Acts 15:1–35), Paul and Barnabas disagreeing over John Mark (Acts 15:36–40), disputes over meat sacrificed to idols (Rom 14), disunity at Corinth (1 Cor 1:10–12), Paul's disagreement with Peter (Gal 2:11–14) and Euodias and Syntyche (Phil 4:2). Further teaching relevant to conflict can be found in Matthew 18:15–20, Luke 22:24–30, Romans 12:16–21, 1

Corinthians 3, Ephesians 2:11–12, 4:31–2, Philippians 2:1–11, Colossians 3:8–14, 2 Timothy 2:14, and James 4:1–12.

CAUSES OF CONFLICT

We have seen that the basic cause of conflict is that we are all different people, with views and approaches that will sooner or later conflict. But there are many other contributory causes to the development of a conflict situation.

1. **Insecurity**, which can lead to the inability to cope with someone who disagrees with you. You are not very sure of yourself or your position and so you assert them all the more vehemently, and attack everyone else's position, lest you should be proved wrong, or they should be proved right.

2. **Oversensitivity**, feeling that rejection of your point of view is a personal rejection of you.

3. **Self-centredness**, causing you to push yourself and your ideas forward and fail to give others respect and acceptance and love.

4. **Prejudice**, over race, class, worship style, age, music, or whatever.

5. **Fear**, of change, or failure, or loss of control.

6. **Bad organization and bad communication.** Most church activities are run by volunteers who are not always expert at organization and communication, providing a fertile breeding ground for misunderstanding and frustration.

7. **The speed of change**, which is particularly threatening to some.

8. **The failure to distinguish between major and minor issues.** It is not just the Pharisees who have problems with gnats and camels. So often Christians have fought each other over matters which, when we look back, are seen to be pretty trivial – whether we should sing hymns or just Psalms, whether we should allow a cross in our building, whether or not the organ is the Devil's instrument, to name just a few that have split Baptist churches in the past. Doubtless many of the issues that are today splitting churches will turn out to be as unimportant in the long run. A useful rule of thumb to adopt is "Is it worth dying for?". If it isn't, then it isn't worth fighting for.

9. **Tired, overburdened church workers**, who when they are on top of things can cope well enough, but who give way under the last straw.

10. **The wiles of the Devil**, who has a vested interest in setting us all against each other.

11. **Personality clash**, arising from a failure to appreciate how different our personalities are, and what an enriching thing that difference can be.

PERSONALITY TYPES

A number of different ways of analysing personality types have been put forward, perhaps the best known approach being that of the Myers-Briggs Personality Type Indicator. The approaches don't all agree in every aspect, but they do vividly illustrate the wide variety there is in personality types.

An appreciation that personality type can be very influential in forming our attitudes and preferences, and sometimes even our beliefs, is a great help towards understanding how conflicts arise. It was a point vividly illustrated on an occasion recently when we had put a hundred or so Christian students through the Myers-Briggs test. We asked a group who had come out on the *extrovert* wing and a group who had come out as *introvert* each to prepare a time of worship and then lead us through it. It is not hard to imagine the graphic contrast between the two acts of worship. The significant thing for the students was that differences they had previously tended to explain in terms of the theology of worship, or of charismatic *v* non charismatic, were highlighted as the result of differences in temperament.

The principle of analysing personality works by assuming that each person is at some point on a scale between personality extremes. The more complex approaches take several scales and work out interesting combinations.

- *Extrovert … Introvert.* We are all at some point between being extremely outwardly orientated and extremely inwardly orientated.

- *Low responsiveness … High responsiveness.* Some of us are little affected by other people or situations while others are quickly and profoundly influenced or even controlled.

- *High assertiveness … Low assertiveness.* Some stand out in a crowd whereas others are easy to ignore.

- *Neuroticism … Emotional stability.* None of us is entirely free from worry, stress, and swings in our emotions, but some are much nearer emotional stability than others.

- *Practical … Imaginative.* Some feel most at home with things which are here and now, measurable, following established routines, often in considerable detail. Others are more interested in the wood than the trees, in dreaming big dreams, and following ideas.

- *Logic … Intuition.* Some like to think things through, analyse, argue according to principles, make carefully thought out decisions whilst others jump to a decision on a hunch, or a feeling, responding personally and intuitively rather than rationally.

As well as the position an individual occupies on specific scales, differing combinations of positions on the various scales can make for specific personality traits. Thus, in a traditional personality analysis, a combination of low assertiveness and high responsiveness will make a *melancholic*, someone who is gifted, artistic, hard-working, and at the same time moody and likely to suffer from a low self image. A person who combines high assertiveness and low responsiveness is likely to be strong willed and get things done, but lacking in sensitivity to other people's needs, making her a good leader to follow, if you can cope with her!

None of the approaches to personality analysis are perfect. I tend to feel that human personalities are so complex that however many boxes we may tick in a questionnaire we can never get everything neatly tied up. The basic lesson , however, is well established. There are dozens, maybe hundreds, of different types of personality. We don't all see things the same way, we don't all respond to data the same way and we don't all make decisions the same way. Little wonder, then, that we disagree! Accepting that we have different personalities and different starting points can be a great help in understanding and dealing with the conflicts that result.

Perhaps the most significant point of all is the realisation that there is no one personality which is *right*, and by which all other personalities are judged wrong. A person is as much *right* in being, say, extrovert or intuitive as another person is in being introvert or wanting to sort everything out logically, just as they are as much *right* in being fair-haired or dark-haired. It is the way that they are. They may not be the same as me or as the person next to them, but we accept them as they are, and find enrichment in their distinct traits. As a consequence, there is no *right* way, say, of worshipping God, for example the extrovert way, that makes all other ways wrong, nor is there a *right* way of making a decision, say, the logically worked out way, that makes the other ways all wrong. *Right* and *wrong* don't apply at personality level – they only come into play when we ask questions like "Is God truly being worshipped?" or "Have we made the right decision?".

CONFLICT DEVELOPMENT

Conflicts never follow set patterns, but here is an outline of how a conflict might develop in a church situation.

1. A and B belong to the same church, but differ widely in their backgrounds, personalities, and way of doing things. For the most part they manage to co-exist, concealing (and perhaps bottling up) their disagreements and annoyance.

2. Something happens – a trigger event or situation – which allows the annoyance, frustration, fear and anger that have been dormant to take shape and find expression.

3. Tension begins, and the conflict becomes public.

4. A and B now each have to justify the stance taken, to demonstrate that one is in the right and the other is wrong. To do this they will try a number of tacks:

   - They will probably feel the need to demonstrate that the issue is not a petty one, but worth taking a firm stand on – 'the thin end of the wedge'.

   - Very often they will each seek to provide theological justification for their stances: "It isn't just a matter of me being awkward over the type of songs we sing, or the Bible version we use; there is a theological issue at stake here". Fighting for theological orthodoxy sounds so much better than being cussed over personal preferences!

   - Consciously or unconsciously one will look for further material which shows that the other person is unreliable, unChristian, etc, thus justifying the attitude taken to the trigger event.

- Each will seek to draw in other people as allies on their side. It is much more secure to have a group around you telling you how right you are in what you are doing than to fight a lone battle!

5. As escalation continues the attack tends to be centred less on the issues and more on the person: "I seriously doubt whether she can really be a Christian"; "The church will never go forward while she is on the leadership team".

6. Case building continues and trenches are dug. To bolster their positions both A and B increasingly overstate their case and the errors of the other side. No longer is it just that the rock band is unsuitable for Sunday worship, now all rock music (not to mention the musicians!) is of the Devil.

7. The conflict escalates to the point where nothing short of the elimination of the other person or group by resignation or a church split will suffice.

CONFLICT RESOLUTION

The counsellor's aim is more than to bring the conflict to a close, and to repair the damage done. It is, as far as is possible, to ensure that out of the whole experience comes creative growth; that at the end of the process the individuals and the church are stronger and further forward in the purposes of God than when the conflict first began. This growth could be in three areas:

1. **Growth over the specific issue that gave rise to the conflict**, for example a dispute over the use of a band in worship leads to a deeper understanding of what worship is all about.

2. **Personal growth**, involving a deeper understanding of ourselves and others, and how we function, closer relationships as a result of having

72

broken fellowship and then being reconciled, and more spiritual maturity.

3. **Growth in understanding and experience of Christian principles and of the power of the gospel.** Ours is the way of love and grace and in Christ there is reconciliation. Apparently insoluble problems can be solved, bad relationships can be healed, conflict can lead to growth and blessing and the Devil doesn't have to have the last laugh.

MEDIATION

Conflicts that are still on a relatively small scale will hopefully not need a mediator, as the pattern outlined in Matthew 18 suggests. But the help of a mediator can be crucial, especially when the conflict is becoming serious. Besides being as neutral as possible, and acceptable to both sides, the mediator will need to be wise, to inspire trust, to be able to exercise the right degree of authority and leadership, and, above all, able to bring the grace and power of Christ into the situation. She is not an ACAS official, but a minister of Christ.

Steps towards conflict resolution could include:

1. Helping the people concerned to see that there is a problem, and that something needs to be done about it. This isn't always as easy as it sounds; frequently self-justification is at such a pitch that the attitude is "There's no problem as far as I'm concerned; it's the other person". The counsellor will need to take care not to apportion blame in any way, being willing perhaps to say something like: "I accept it may not be your problem, but the situation is such that damage is being done to the church, and you are a key person to help do something about it".

2. Lift the whole thing from the level of a quarrel over some issue or a clash of personalities to that of: "What is God saying to us in this situation, and what does he want to do?". Pray with the individuals concerned; if you can manage it, get them together to pray. An evening of waiting upon the Lord together in prayer may accomplish far more than hours of discussion of the issues.

3. Where necessary, help the people concerned to acknowledge the value of different personalities and approaches, and how we can enrich one another by each making our distinctive contribution. Stress that God

has allowed this conflict to arise so that we may all grow and go forward as a result. Gently remind them of the key virtues of grace and humility, forbearance and love, and of Bible teaching like Romans 14 where Paul in fact asks the stronger Christian, the one whose position seems to be the most theologically correct, to be the one who gives way.

4. Get those concerned to start talking about the issues, hopefully face to face, or, if necessary, through the mediator. This is important in order to locate and clarify the real issues, but it can become tedious and even counterproductive if it develops into further arguments over who said or did what, and when. It is therefore vitally important that the main thrust of the discussion should not be "What actually happened at some time in the past?", but "What is God saying to us now about the present and the future, as we bring both the negatives and the positives of the past before him, and how are we going to make sure that out of this situation comes growth and enrichment and blessing?".

5. Where issues do need to be analysed and talked through, it may be wise to establish ground rules for procedure, similar to those we were looking at in the last unit. Issues may fall into various categories:

- **Issues of fact.** If facts can be established relatively easily (eg who actually had booked the hall when the Ladies' Keep Fit turned up to find a Youth Group riot in progress), well and good; responsibility can be accepted, apologies made, and a better system for booking the hall introduced. Facts, however, are rarely facts alone, they are often overlaid with feelings (there might not have been the same angry reaction if it had been the Mums and Toddlers occupying the hall), and, as we have seen, facts can be so complex that it just is not worth the effort trying to find them.

- **Issues of theology.** Even though it may be true that theology has only been dragged in to bolster a position adopted for other reasons, most Christian counsellors will feel the need to take theological issues seriously. Here are some suggestions:

  a. Accept (and help them to accept) that each side has valuable theological insights. Each has some truth (possibly mixed, of course, with a bit of error) and has a right to hold that position. They are not being deliberately perverse, or consciously twisting scripture to their own end. God is speaking to and through both of them, and the whole church needs to be enriched by what he is saying.

b. Find as much theological common ground as possible; prise them gently away from extremes to an acknowledgement of how much middle ground there is. For example, in a controversy over Signs and Wonders, help the parties to see that the anti-Signs and Wonders people still believe that God answers prayer and does miracles, though not necessarily in very spectacular ways; while the other side doesn't actually believe that every service should be regularly punctuated with blinding flashes of light and raising of the dead.

c. Seek to show that theological disagreement does not entail separation or even conflict. In Baptist churches even a major issue like baptism need not divide. In many churches those baptised as believers and those not baptised as believers work happily together with no tension.

d. If necessary, try to find an agreed statement of theology that both sides can accept as a temporary working base. Personally I'm not keen on something that will bind the church for the next few centuries. It is better to say that this is a statement of what we believe the Lord is saying to us now, and that we are open to him to lead us on further in due course.

- **Issues of policy**. Quite often it will be right to upgrade what starts as a squabble over a petty issue into a matter of the vision or policy of the church. To put it on its lowest level, this justifies the people concerned for making a fuss, but it is also a matter of listening to the voice of God through any circumstance. A squabble over the use of drama in the service can therefore give rise to a major review of what we are doing and what we should be doing when we meet together on Sundays. Such a review, of course, will need to be conducted by the whole church, perhaps through house groups, discussion groups or a week-end conference, but giving due attention to the immediate issues that have provoked it. Similarly, a conflict over, say, the role of women in church leadership should not be resolved by an ad hoc decision, but by the whole church together seeking God's guidance on the issue, preferably over a substantial period of time, in order to take the heat out of the specific conflict situation. Again, I would urge that policy decisions made in this way should not be looked on as binding for all time, but as an expression of God's guidance for the immediate future.

- **Issues of attitude.** Attitudes are not easy to change, and, confronted with deeply entrenched attitudes, the counsellor may be able to do little more than teach the virtues of acceptance and forbearance. If she or he does try to change attitudes, it will be worth remembering:

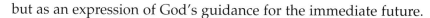

  a. An attitude which has developed over many years is not likely to vanish overnight. Rather, it may be a matter of developing that attitude in a new and positive direction.

  b. It can be useful to make a point of helping the person to distinguish clearly between their attitude to the issue and their attitude to the person, hating the sin, maybe, but loving the sinner.

  c. Wrong attitudes breed on ignorance and misinformation. Seek to break down barriers by correcting false beliefs and encouraging close contact with those on the other side.

- **Issues of feelings.** Don't dismiss people's feelings; they may seem trivial or mistaken to us, but they are very real to them. If the older people in the church feel pushed out, or the youngsters feel they don't get a fair hearing, take these feelings seriously. Listen, get others to listen, and find ways of dealing with the issues raised, or helping the individuals to cope with their feelings.

6. Seek to bring the people concerned to full reconciliation, asking for and receiving forgiveness from each other and the Lord. Though a public reconciliation and confession of failings can be very beneficial for the church and individuals, remember that imperfect human beings, even though they are Christians, may need a degree of 'face saving'. We don't need to go to the extent the managers and the trade unionists do who both need to claim that the settlement is a victory for them. Equally, it is not our desire to humiliate anyone, and the easier we make it for them to give ground and set the antagonisms of the past behind them, the better. If a positive outcome has come from the conflict, it need not be hypocritical even to express gratitude to all the parties for bringing the issues forward. All this can help set the individuals and the church fellowship up to go forward on a positive note, leaving behind them the failings and negatives of the past.

UNIT 7
LOW SELF-IMAGE

At the root of many problems the counsellor will meet is a low or a negative self-image, a phrase I am using to cover a cluster of conditions ranging from insecurity to self-rejection. Though symptoms can, of course, arise from other sources, frequently low self-image lies at the root of conditions as diverse as anorexia and excessive eating, withdrawal and aggression, depression and attention seeking.

The problem is symptomatic of our society; other cultures don't seem to have encountered it anywhere near as much as we do. It is hard to think of any Bible teaching on the subject. Indeed, it could be argued that the Bible's emphasis is all the other way, attacking high self-esteem in the form of pride, self-assertion and self-confidence. From this we might conclude that the Bible's teaching is that a low self-image is not a bad thing; alternatively, we might decide that in biblical times low self-esteem was far less of a problem than it is for us today. In the culture of the Bible the sources from which individuals gained self-worth were generally well in place – the secure family unit, an accepting local community, the sense of being the chosen and loved people of God. All these contributed strongly to a sense of belonging, and being accepted, of security and self-worth.

In our society so many of the foundational structures which we need to give us security have been broken down. Many people have missed out on a secure family background, the sense of being wanted or belonging, or being affirmed and accepted as they grew up. In the competitive atmosphere of so much of our culture, acceptance has come to depend on achievement, financially or academically, being popular, being 'in', being good at sport, or good looking, or being up to date with the latest fashions – all things which are hard to sustain, and providing an insecure foundation on which to build an understanding of who we are. Rejection, brokenness and insecurity are all hallmarks of much of our society: from these sources come low self-image.

SOURCES OF LOW SELF-IMAGE

Once again, given the complexity of so many of the people who come to us for help, the counsellor may not be able to provide a definitive analysis of where the person's lack of self-worth comes from. That need not prevent him going forward with counselling and ministry. There is, however, value in gaining an understanding of the source, if this is possible. Not only will it help the person to be aware that his low self-esteem is something caused by external forces, and therefore something that can be changed by countering those external forces, but it will also help the counsellor and the person to decide on the best way of seeking to do just that.

1. Inadequate relationships in early life

A baby or a young child needs above all to be loved, accepted, and nurtured. If this need is not met an unconscious pattern may develop: "Others reject me. Therefore I am to be rejected. Therefore I reject myself". Alternatively there may be a defence mechanism: "Being rejected hurts. I cannot stand the pain of others rejecting me. Therefore I will reject myself before they reject me, in order to lessen the hurt".

Rejection in early life can take many forms. Perhaps the most common is the conscious or unconscious rejection of the child, in the womb or subsequently, because the parents did not want the pregnancy. Alternatively, the child is the wrong sex, or has a physical handicap or learning difficulties, or does not live up to the parents' expectations. Rejection by one or both parents may come as the result of tension in the home or marriage break up. Over-ambitious parents who, perhaps because of their own insecurity, desperately need the child to 'succeed', may demand high standards, giving little affirmation or praise, and ending up instilling into the growing child a sense that he will never be able to achieve what is expected of him.

2. Lack of affirmation

We learn to affirm ourselves by being affirmed by others. The primary source of affirmation is our parents and immediate family. Other sources are our friends, peer group, and success in the areas our culture thinks are important. Particularly in adolescence, but also in childhood and adulthood, all sorts of questions and self-doubt arise: "Who am I? Am I 'normal'? Do I like myself? Do others like me?", and so on. Continuous negative responses to such questions can have a devastating effect.

3. Lack of security

Again, the ideal, as pictured in the Bible, is that every person should belong to a secure family unit, and should live, each 'under his own vine and under his own fig-tree' (Micah 4:4), confident in the love and grace and provision of God. By contrast, for many, insecurity is the hallmark of life, whether in the home, or in the field of employment, or in the collapse of the structures of society. Not only do we have to cope with external insecurity, it has invaded the sphere of ideas and principles. Former generations believed that there was such a thing as fixed unchanging truth; facts that we could know and be sure of. Additionally, right and wrong, good and bad, were for the most part fixed and agreed by all. Our generation, however, lives in an age of relativism. Nothing can be known for sure and there is no agreement on what is right and wrong, good and bad. Principles, standards, parameters have all disappeared. For some this may bring a feeling of release, of welcome freedom, of throwing off chains of bondage. For many it is immensely threatening. It casts us adrift in a sea of darkness, with no hope of finding fixed land. Straightforward beliefs and simple faith may have marked former generations – ours is characterized by fear and doubt. Even for committed Christians, a steady faith in God is often very hard to sustain, especially when faced with the scepticism of an unbelieving world. All these insecurities – structural, mental and spiritual – press in upon us, leading to loss of trust in things and people and life in general. Uncertainty, doubt and fear characterize our thinking, and seek to destroy any confidence or trust we may have in God or in ourselves.

4. A false understanding of Christian teaching

Biblical phrases about 'denying ourselves', 'humbling ourselves', and 'putting other people first', and non-biblical concepts like 'we are miserable sinners', 'the body is evil', and 'to avoid pride we must hate ourselves', can all contribute to a negative view of ourselves.

Theologians have debated whether the concept of encouraging people to adopt a positive self-image, which has come into Christian thinking from secular psychology, is in keeping with biblical teaching about humility and the denying of self. Some argue that the biblical emphasis is strongly weighted towards the need to put down self, to resist the pressure towards pride and self-confidence. Others, while accepting the Bible's call to humility, point out that it also calls us to a realistic view of ourselves ('with sober judgment' Rom 12:3), to valuing ourselves as made in the image of God and redeemed by the blood of Christ, and even perhaps to self-love ('love your neighbour as *yourself*' Matt 19:19).

This is probably not an issue which can be solved by quoting a few proof texts. We have already seen that the Bible was addressing a different cultural situation than the one we face today. Perhaps the answer to the debate is to develop a concept of self-acceptance and self-esteem which is totally in keeping with the Bible's teaching on self-denial and humility. There seems no reason why this should not be possible. We have to go no further than the life of Jesus to find a perfect example of deep humility expressed in submission and obedience to God and in service to others, combined with self-acceptance and a realistic understanding of who he was and what he was called by God to do. If a positive self-image follows some secular psychologies into assertiveness and the self-deceit implicit in some forms of 'positive thinking', then of course it is wrong. If it can sit happily with all the biblical material that is there to keep us from the sin of pride and to make us more Christlike, then it can be accepted.

RESULTS OF LOW SELF-IMAGE

1. Personal

Someone with a low self-image will only be able to see the negatives about himself. Whatever positives there may be, however much others may seek to affirm or compliment him, he will be unable to accept it. In its milder forms, this may appear simply as humility; in its more pronounced forms it will give rise to discouragement, a sense of uselessness, self-fulfilling prophecies of failure, and a downward spiral into withdrawal, depression and hopelessness.

2. Relationships

The inability to accept and love oneself can lead to the inability to accept and love others, and the inability to receive acceptance and love from others. Both of these result in serious problems in forming relationships.

Even if a relationship has been formed, a person with a low self-image will often have difficulty in maintaining it. There will be a strong tendency to anticipate that the relationship will not last, and this frequently precipitates attitudes and actions which cause the relationship to fail. What is true of human relationships applies also to the relationship with God. This person finds it desperately hard to accept the truths of God's love, forgiveness, unconditional acceptance, and so on.

Some people will express their low self-image or sense of insecurity by becoming hyperactive, or excessively assertive and aggressive. This is the 'argument weak here; shout all the louder' syndrome. To avoid the pain of other people realising how inadequate they are, or to avoid admitting this to themselves, they seek to demonstrate to everybody that they can achieve, they are winners and not failures. A similar pattern can be seen in someone who is judgmental and critical of others. Rather than admit that he has a problem he consciously or unconsciously seeks to show that it is the other person who is in some way inadequate.

3. Physical

Low self-image can lead to rejection or abuse of the body. Two common forms this takes are eating disorders and sexual problems. In anorexia it can be that the person is expressing hatred of the body by starving and even killing it. In over-eating it may be that he is unconsciously highlighting his failure, in that he cannot control his eating. Sexual problems may take the form of the rejection of sexuality in sexual tension and frigidity, or the rejection of gender, or the abuse of sexuality in promiscuity or perversion. Again, we need to remember that these symptoms may have other sources; it is not right to assume that an eating disorder or a sexual problem is necessarily the result of low self-image. Even though it may be one of the most common, low self-image is only one possible source among many.

4. Spiritual

Not only may a Christian who suffers from a low self-image find difficulty in relating to God and to other Christians, he is likely to be a poor witness to the peace and joy and transforming power of the gospel. His basic sense of failure can spill over into his Christian life, leading to lack of growth and general ineffectiveness, and the downward spiral that ends up concluding that Christianity itself is a failure.

1. Recognise the problem

In one person the presenting problem may be depression, and in another an eating disorder, in another aggression. If the counsellor should come to suspect that low self-worth is at the root of these presenting problems, then he will need to probe gently, observing carefully the attitudes the person has towards himself, how he talks about himself, treats himself, handles his failures, and so on. While direct questions are best avoided, requests like, "Tell me about how you got on with your parents when you were a child" can help to open up issues.

Once the counsellor is reasonably sure about the source of the problem the analysis can be shared with the person, helping him to see that his basic problem is not the presenting issue, but something that is emotional, subjective, and in fact false – a wrong feeling, attitude or belief about himself.

Martin, one of the church's pastoral counsellors, was approached by Tony, one of the deacons, who asked if he would talk to Sally, his wife. Though a gifted and capable person, she had recently given up her job on the grounds that it was causing her stress, had subsequently stopped driving the car "because the traffic was getting too heavy", was now talking of giving up her youth leadership job, which she normally loved doing, "because she couldn't cope", and was beginning to avoid people and shut herself up at home. Martin agreed to see her, with Tony there as well.

Martin's first thought was that Sally was suffering from exhaustion, even burnout, but it became clear this was not so. She was not generally stressed, and they had recently had a refreshing holiday. Nor was there a physical explanation, she had recently had a medical check up and was in the best of health. She did not appear to be depressed, and her spiritual life seemed to be fine.

It was when she started talking about what Martin recognized as the trigger event, giving up her job, that clues began to emerge. All had been well until she made just one mistake in compiling a set of figures. This made the whole set wrong, put her boss in an embarrassing situation at the board meeting and he had responded by taking his anger out on her in no uncertain way. It became clear that her subsequent pattern of withdrawal was in reaction to this incident.

Asked why she reacted in such an extreme way to one isolated event, Sally replied that the things her boss had shouted at her in his anger, that she was stupid and useless, were in fact the truth. The capable, successful Sally the people in the church knew, was just a facade, a pretence at coping. The real Sally had never coped, and never would cope; she had always been a failure. Tony agreed that much of Sally's 'coping' was a front and all through their marriage she had struggled with feelings of inadequacy and failure. In fact she could never remember a time when she hadn't known she was stupid and useless.

2. Metanoia

This is a great New Testament word, often translated 'repentance', but literally meaning 'a change of mind'. It has a rich range of relevant applications.

- **Repentance and forgiveness.** In that the person will already be feeling pretty bad about himself, it is not appropriate to start emphasizing his sin. Even so, a crucial first stage is the acknowledgement that what he has been believing about himself may not necessarily be true. It may be something that has been inculcated into him since childhood, but if it is not true, then it is false, and falsehoods are things which as Christians we need deliberately to turn away from, so that we can find and live the truth. The counsellor should sensitively help the person to get to the point where he admits that he may have got it wrong, and to seek God's forgiveness and healing for any area in which he has accepted and followed lies about himself.

- **Thinking biblically.** The second stage of *metanoia* is seeking to change our thinking into what is true. For this there is no better place to start than the Bible. The person may well be familiar with the Bible passages which condemn them; the counsellor will seek to stress the more positive passages, which will help to correct their lack of balance.

83

In trying to help Sally to escape from the low self-image that dominated all her thinking, Martin took her through three foundational biblical truths, illustrating each one from scripture, getting her to read and assimilate relevant passages.

1. **God knows the truth about us.** He knows everything. He knows us better than we know ourselves. He knows the whole picture, the real picture. We may be mistaken but he never is. Among scriptures Martin used were Psalm 139:1–4, John 1:44–51, Hebrews 2:12–13, and 1 John 3:19–20. Sally was quite willing to accept these scriptures, but still maintained her belief that all there was to be known about her was negative.

2. **God loves us, accepts us, and values us as we are.** Martin picked out three specific Bible verses to press these three points home. He got Sally to read and learn them and talked about them, unpacking their meaning and implications. They were Romans 5:8, stressing God's unconditional love; Romans 15:7, teaching his acceptance; and 1 Peter 1:18–19, emphasizing the great value God places on each on of us. He illustrated them by referring to familiar Bible stories like the lost sheep, to Jesus' attitude towards the woman taken in adultery, and towards Peter after he had denied him, thus helping Sally to see that just as Jesus did not reject these, he does not reject her. As Sally began to grasp this, Martin led her on to see that, if God knows the truth about her, and out of that knowledge comes love, acceptance, and valuing, then these three things must form the basis for the right and appropriate way of thinking about Sally. "God sees me this way; since God has got to be right, if I see myself rightly, I must see myself the same way as God sees me; and anyone who sees me differently has got it wrong". Giving verbal assent to this was not too difficult for Sally, but Martin was fully aware that thought patterns she had followed for years, even decades, were not that easy to break.

3. **God calls and equips us for effective Christian living.** In his love and grace, God undertakes to give us all we need to be the people he wants us to be, and to do the things he wants us to do. Martin used Ephesians 1:3–4, the parable of the talents in Matthew 25:14–30, and Paul's teaching about the Holy Spirit's gifts in 1 Corinthians 12, to help Sally to grasp this. He encouraged her to accept it as the truth about herself, not because she felt it, but because God says it. She was able to do this, though still very hesitantly, knowing that her head knowledge was still very liable to be swamped by her feelings.

- **The renewing of the mind.** The counsellor has to counter years of ingrained negative thought patterns. Prayer and the ministry of the Holy Spirit are foundational here as is commitment and hard work on the part of the person being counselled. It is a question of 'taking captive every thought to make it obedient to Christ' (2 Cor 10:5).

Techniques can be helpful, for example writing Bible verses such as Colossians 2:9–10, Ephesians 2:6–10, and Philippians 4:13 on cards and putting them in prominent places where they can be seen. Keeping a journal, or having a regular commitment to open analysis of thought patterns with the counsellor or a close friend, can be a stimulus to progress.

3. Dealing with the root causes

Where it has been possible to analyse root causes of the low self-image, the counsellor will seek to deal with these. This will need to be done on at least two levels.

- Where there has been an inadequate relationship, or lack of affirmation, or a significantly insecure childhood, the counsellor will encourage the person to talk through his feelings about these things, leading him to the point where where he is able to bring them to the Lord, with all his attendant anger and resentment, seeking healing, and the grace to forgive those who were responsible for the wrong. Through the power of the Holy Spirit, the hold of these things can be broken.

- The counsellor will also seek to replace the affirmation and security the person has lacked with positive experiences in the present and future. Above all this will arise out of a living and developing relationship with God, in which the person experiences what it is to be accepted and loved by him, but it also needs to be mirrored in positive relationships with other people. Hopefully the church family will provide soil in which this kind of relationship of loving acceptance and trust can grow.

During his conversations with Sally, it became clear to Martin that her relationship with her father had been a major influence in the development of her low self-image. For as long as she could remember, she had longed to have her father's approval, but somehow or other he had never been able to show this, or to give her praise. Instead, he was continually critical, telling her she was stupid and a failure. When as a small child she did drawings for him, he laughed at them; when she tried her hand at cooking he made rude remarks about the results. Again and again he compared her unfavourably with others, and assured her that she would never get married, because no man would ever want her as his wife.

Confronted with this Martin sought first of all to help Sally to see if the things that her father had said were true or not. In many cases, she was able to accept that they were not. In any case, however great her respect for her father, she had already accepted that God's view of her was more to be believed than even her father's.

Next, as they talked together, Martin helped Sally explore possible reasons for her father's attitude. Did he reject Sally because she was a girl? Or was he an insecure person or a failure himself, and couldn't cope with anyone else being secure or succeeding? Was his attitude part of a power struggle within the marriage, whereby her mother always took her side, and her father always attacked her? In the end Sally decided that the most likely analysis was that her father was an ambitious man; he had not met with much success himself and clearly felt the need to succeed through the success of his children. Her elder brother seemed to do everything right; he was bright, good looking, and successful. She, on the other hand, developed later, and by the time she started to succeed her father had developed his negative pattern of relating to her, and couldn't change it without much loss of face.

Becoming aware of the source of her father's attitude helped Sally realise how unjust and false it was, and thus to escape from its influence. Martin used a time of prayer ministry to confirm this, and encouraged Sally to forgive her father for the wrong he had done her. She found this very hard to do. Even when she thought she had managed it, feelings of resentment soon came flooding back. Martin encouraged her not to be too worried about this, but to take the resentment to the Lord whenever it occurred, knowing that there was sufficient grace to cope with it all. The two agreed that it would be inappropriate to confront her father with the wrongness of his attitude to his daughter, or, indeed, to go to him and say "I forgive you". Instead, Martin encouraged Sally to seek to develop as positive a relationship as she could with her father, aided by the fuller insights she had gained into his personality, and seeking the healing and renewing power of the Holy Spirit in the minds of them both.

4. Paraclesis

We mentioned briefly the New Testament word *paraclesis* in Unit 2. It is a word I particularly like, because Jesus used it to refer to the ministry of both himself and the Holy Spirit in John 14:16. The NIV translates it 'counsellor' but it could as easily be translated 'encourager'. Its meaning is made clear by 1 Thessalonians 5:11: 'Therefore *encourage* one another and build each other up, just as in fact you are doing'. Faced with the brokenness, neurosis, insecurity, fear, doubt and loss of love in so many people's lives, the ministry of paraclesis is likely to be one of the main tasks of the contemporary Christian counsellor, whether or not low self image is the main diagnosis in a given counselling situation. Through love, prayer, the ministry of the Holy Spirit, and the sensitive teaching of biblical truth, the counsellor will seek to enable the person to grow, encouraging and building up the work that God is already doing in him (2 Tim 1:7). Hopefully, too, the wider church will share in the ministry of paraclesis, in particular, perhaps, through a supportive house group.

5. Changing the focus

Low self-image can at times be a very self-obsessed thing. While he is in a sense rejecting it, self with its failures and worthlessness in fact becomes the centre of the person's world. Where this happens, the counsellor will need to direct attention away from self, perhaps by giving him someone else to think about and minister to. There may be a dear old lady who needs visiting, who will not make demands, but rather will be genuinely appreciative, thus helping the person to take his eyes off himself and find self-worth in service. True Christian humility is not rejecting self, but forgetting self in service of others.

6. Patience

We have already noted that patterns of thought which have been deeply ingrained for years generally take time to change. This may especially be the case where the motivation to change is not high, for example where the patterns of behaviour arising from the low self-image supply the person with gratifying attention. Necessarily, too, someone with a low self-image will be subject to discouragement, and to giving up the effort to change. All this calls for patience, and the ability to cope with setbacks and apparent lack of progress.

UNIT 8
CHILD ABUSE

In our final unit we are looking at a fairly specialized topic which is increasingly coming to the attention of counsellors. Once again, as we go through it, we will seek to illustrate the application of some of the principles outlined in the early units.

The term *child abuse* covers any action by someone who has power over a child that is damaging to him or her. This includes:

- *Physical abuse.* It was not until the 1960s that the extent of physical abuse of children was recognized, from 'battered babies' upwards. The NSPCC reckons that over 150 children die every year at the hands of their parents.

- *Sexual abuse.* Before the 1980s reports of child sexual abuse were usually dismissed as fantasy or malice. It is now recognized that it is widespread, and has been for some considerable time.

- *Emotional abuse.* Shouting, taunting, threats, rejection etc are increasingly being recognized as potentially very damaging.

- *Ritual abuse.* This covers various forms of organized abuse, frequently linked with sexual abuse, for example by a paedophile gang. As yet few accept the existence of religious ritual abuse by satanists and the like. Corroborated evidence and convictions are both very hard to get in this kind of area.

We will be concentrating on *sexual* abuse in this unit.

Statistics on child sexual abuse vary greatly, often as a result of differing definitions of what abuse is. Technically, abuse is a very wide term, including exposure or the touching of primary or secondary sexual parts of the body. The number of children subjected to such abuse, perhaps on a one-off occasion, is likely to be high – one report suggested over 50%. If, however, abuse is taken in its narrower sense of involving some form of intercourse over a period of time, the figure could be between 3% and 10% of all children. Girls are considerably more at risk than boys. Abuse can be perpetrated by siblings or other children. Though some may be by strangers, the great majority of abuse is by people the child knows well, relatives, babysitters, and especially fathers and stepfathers. Almost all adult abusers are male. There appears to be no regional variation. More cases come to light in socially disadvantaged groups, but it may be the case that other classes are better able to conceal what is happening. Hopefully its frequency is less among Christians and in churches, but we need to be aware that people with weaknesses in this area may well find themselves attracted to church youth work.

Abuse can start at any age, perhaps beginning in a small way, but developing to regular intercourse and extending over a long period. Pressure is put on the child not to tell, perhaps through threats of violence, or promise of reward, or the fear that daddy will be sent to prison if they tell. Many children hate the experience, but others may enjoy the attention it gives them and the rewards it brings. In father/daughter situations the mother will often know what is happening but will be afraid to do anything about it for fear of the consequences.

POSSIBLE INDICATIONS OF ABUSE

Should there be some risk that a child is being abused, it may be appropriate to watch out for some of these indications, though, of course, the existence of these things in themselves is no proof of abuse.

- Changes in mood or behaviour, particularly where a child withdraws, regresses, starts underachieving, or becomes clingy, for no apparent reason.

- Inappropriate relationship with peers or adults.

- Injuries which are not readily explained, or have not received medical attention.

- Inappropriate sexual knowledge in the child, or pre-occupation with sexual matters. Sexual play or talk – a child may even be sexually provocative with adults.

- Persistent tiredness; bad dreams possibly with sexual connotations.

WHEN A CHILD WANTS TO TALK ABOUT ABUSE

A decade or so ago it was standard for a child who claimed to be being abused to meet with disbelief. It could be that in reaction to this we have gone too far in the other direction. Some Social Services departments have swung into action, for example arranging for the removal of the

90

father, and taking the children of the family into care, simply on the strength of allegations by one child which have turned out to be untrue. Certainly, it is no longer the case that stories of abuse are simply not the kind of thing a child could make up. Children have access to videos showing child abuse and they learn about it at school – it is an 'in' subject. It is quite possible for them to fantasize or to make mischievous or malicious allegations.

Nevertheless, it is essential, whatever doubts the counsellor may have, to listen seriously to a child who makes any such allegations. If they are being abused, and have been threatened with dire consequences if they tell anyone, then we should do nothing that makes it harder for them to tell. The counsellor must therefore avoid showing signs of shock or incredulity. He or she should listen carefully and accept what the child says. Don't probe, in particular don't say anything that might put thoughts into the child's mind. Don't promise confidentiality, you may well be legally required to pass on the information you are being given. Don't be judgmental; if it is a case of genuine abuse it is important that the child gets the message that she has done the right thing in talking about it.

After the conversation write down what the child has said as fully as you can remember. Whatever doubts you may have about the truth of the allegations, the next step is to pass what you have been told on to someone in the church, perhaps the minister or the youth pastor, who will help you decide what to do with it. If the allegations are of serious abuse and there are grounds for believing that they are true, and particularly if the abuse is continuing or other children are at risk, the authorities must be informed through an NSPCC officer or the local Social Services department. If there is serious doubt about the truth of the allegations, every effort should be made to decide the issue one way or the other; it should not just be left unresolved.

HELPING A CHILD WHO HAS BEEN ABUSED

Once the authorities have been informed, much of the responsibility may well be taken out of your hands. However, even if the child is being seen by a specialist counsellor, the Christian counsellor or others in the church may still have a significant role to play, supplementing the work of the professional. Here are some points to bear in mind.

1. Sadly, the immediate results of a child telling about abuse, particularly if the abuse is by a close family member, can be more frightening than the abuse itself. It involves the intrusion of all sorts of people into the family, and quite possibly causes the family to be broken up. This can be terrifying and the child will need continuing love and care and support and reassurance.

2. A child who has been abused by an adult in a position of trust may find it hard to trust other adults. Additionally, if official processes are going forward, the child will find herself being confronted with further potentially frightening adults such as police officers and social workers. It is especially important, therefore, that the counsellor and other adults in the church should take special care to build wholesome and trusting relationships with the child.

3. The child may need help over feelings of guilt, either because she feels that she was partly responsible for the abuse taking place, or that she has brought about more disasters by telling about the abuse.

4. Where the abuser is the father, care should be taken to prevent the relationship between the child and the father being completely destroyed. In talking about him the counsellor may be able to point out that though what he did was very wrong, in many respects he was a good father; nobody's father is perfect and they all make mistakes, though perhaps not so serious as this particular one. The familiar point about care over talk about God as father comes in here. My own feeling is that the biblical concept is so rich that we should not abandon talk of God as father simply because a child has had a bad experience of her own father. Care should be taken to define fatherhood in terms of God rather than God in terms of our earthly fathers.

5. Abuse can give rise to a number of problems, often some time after the experience. Some of these may be dealt with by the child psychologist. The counsellor should be aware of the possibility of such things as bad dreams, guilt, fear of adults, low self-worth, fear of sex, overemphasis on sex, and insecurity, and should be able to give sensitive counselling and prayer ministry where appropriate.

6. In situations where the child is confused over what is right and wrong in the sexual area, possibly as the result of being exposed to pornographic videos and the like, careful explanation of what is and what is not acceptable may be required.

HELPING ADULTS WHO HAVE BEEN ABUSED AS CHILDREN

Some adults who have gone through the experience of childhood sexual abuse have learnt to cope with the experience and have few problems as a result. Many, however, continue to struggle with bad memories, guilt, anger, feelings of powerlessness and betrayal, or show disturbing patterns of behaviour, or experience specific problems arising from the abuse. Such symptoms could include:

- The inability to trust, especially, in the case of female victims, the inability to trust men.

- Difficulty in showing or receiving affection and love.

- Low self-image, self-rejection, rejection of or abuse of the body. They have been treated as a thing, so they treat themselves as a thing.

- Feelings of uncleanness; looking on sex as dirty; obsessive cleanliness.

- Sexual problems, ranging from frigidity to promiscuity.

SUPPRESSED MEMORIES

There is an ongoing debate on the issue of suppressed memories of childhood sexual abuse. Most people recognize that the pain and trauma of abuse can lead to memories of it, and of other events in the same period, being lost from a person's memory. Thus the fact that someone cannot remember anything about an extended period of her childhood may be an indicator that she was suffering abuse during that period. Again, however, it is not an infallible indicator. There could be other causes of the suppression.

For some years it was generally held that, according to the Freudian model, such suppressed memories can emerge in certain circumstances, in particular as the result of counselling, hypnosis, and the like, and that if they do, they should be taken very seriously. Some Christians exercising forms of 'inner healing' ministry have followed this line of thinking. However, recently several have questioned the wisdom and validity of this approach. Do we need to dredge through the unconscious to find such things? And is not the danger of 'finding' something that is not really there so high as to make the whole exercise invalid?

While I accept there are dangers, and that this approach, like any, can be overdone, my own feeling is that there are some good insights here. Abuse is the kind of thing that can cause suppression of memories; and, while we should not normally go out of our way to try to bring suppressed memories to the surface, in circumstances where an adult has serious problems that could best be explained by childhood sexual abuse, this possibility should at least be explored. Great care, however, should be taken not to project the possibility of abuse falsely into their mind or memory.

Healing will generally be a long process. It will contain elements of:

- **The ability to accept that abuse has taken place.** Quite apart from the issue of suppressed memories, adults who have experienced 'less serious' forms of abuse may play down their significance. They may be unaware that any form of sexual invasion, through touch, nudity or pornography, or even in words, can cause deep traumas, especially if it happens repeatedly, or at a time when the child is particularly sensitive or vulnerable. The counsellor will need to help the person to face and accept the reality both of the abuse and of the damage it has done, the pain and the shame, and the extent to which it has affected her subsequent life.

- **Prayer for cleansing and healing.** Though the feeling of defilement may appear exaggerated, the counsellor needs to accept that both the feeling and the defilement are real, and need to be dealt with. After helping the victim to express these things and her reactions to them, appropriate prayer ministry should be given, seeking the cleansing and healing of the Holy Spirit. The counsellor will need to emphasize that the victim does not need to seek forgiveness for the abuse. God does not hold her responsible even though she may blame herself for it. Nevertheless, where there are persistent feelings of guilt, arising perhaps from the fact that she allowed herself to get into a situation where the abuse could happen, or from the ambivalence that meant she actually enjoyed some aspects of it, these should be brought to the Lord in confession, whether or not the counsellor feels they are justified. Here the counsellor's role is to declare the grace and forgiveness of God, rather than to pass judgment on the validity or otherwise of the guilt feelings. Once again, the counsellor will need to warn the person that feelings of defilement and of guilt may well continue to return, and give help over how to cope with them when they do.

- **Forgiveness of the abuser.** Here the counsellor will need to combine a clear understanding of the need to forgive and the power of expressions of forgiveness, with an awareness that getting to the point of forgiveness may take a very long time, and that even after it has been reached feelings of anger, hatred, bitterness, and so on may continue to return.

- **Spiritual severance from the abuser.** In some cases it may be appropriate to break the psychological and spiritual hold of the abuser and attitudes he has instilled over the victim through prayer and some form of deliverance ministry, provided this is in keeping with the theological understanding both of the counsellor and of the person who has been abused.

- **Dealing with self-rejection, and gaining self-worth.**

- **Help in the areas that have been damaged or perverted by the experience of abuse.**

- **Advice over confronting the abuser and informing the authorities.** The choice in these areas will have to be made by the victim; where the abuse was within the family it may be right to encourage them to consult with other family members. In some cases no useful purpose is likely to be served by taking further action. If there should be any risk that the person is still practising abuse, however, action must be taken.

HELPING ABUSERS

If it is a situation where social workers and police are involved, then they will arrange for professional counselling. Where this does not happen the abuser should still be encouraged to seek specialized help. However, if the task of seeking to counsel and minister to an abuser does fall to you, the same principles can be followed that underly our approaches to counselling in the areas we have looked at in other units:

1. **Enable the abuser to face up to the seriousness of what they have done.** A standard reaction to the accusation of abuse is denial, or attempts to play down the seriousness of the offence. The abuser may produce all sorts of excuses to justify his actions, including blaming the victim for leading him on. The counsellor will need to help him face up to the reality and seriousness of what he has done. Not only is

this a vital step towards repentance and forgiveness, seeing the abuse in all its loathsomeness will hopefully help the person to resist temptations to do it again.

2. **Try to find any underlying causes for his abuse.** Among possible factors is that he was abused himself as a child, he has serious sexual problems, he has a need to express power, or he is under high stress. A common pattern is that of a person who, as a result of low self-image or some other reason, finds it difficult to relate to adults and who turns to children for friendship and acceptance. At first relationships are harmless, but over a period of time they develop in intensity and move into abuse. Once this has happened, the person, plagued with guilt and shame, plunges further into self-rejection and the inability to face other adults, and his continuing desperate need to find love and acceptance leads to further abuse.

   Once again, such is the complexity of the human personality, it may be very hard for the counsellor to unravel with full certainty the true source of a person's problems. Analysing at least some of the probable root causes can help him understand himself better and begin to see what steps he might take towards change. In the case of abuse, in particular, the counsellor will need to stress that factors which have led to abuse do not excuse it. The person at each stage of the process was responsible for the choices he made. There are many others, who, for example, went through the same childhood experiences of rejection which gave rise to a low self-image, who have not given way to the pressure to indulge in abuse.

3. **Repentance and forgiveness.** The counsellor will be aware that repentance must be far deeper than mere remorse or shame at being found out. A specific act of repentance and seeking forgiveness and cleansing, ideally in the presence of a small group of church leaders, can be of great significance, but it should be stressed that true repentance is a continuing process and not just an isolated act. It gives rise to new patterns of thinking and behaving, and needs to be re-applied when the pressure is on to fall back into sin.

   An integral part of repentance is that the abuser should admit his sin to those he has wronged and, where appropriate, ask for their forgiveness. This includes other family members, and those whose trust has been betrayed.

   As with forgiveness in any area, such is the grace and power of the gospel that once the sin has been confessed and turned from, God's forgiveness is total, however strong the feelings of defilement and shame may be that remain. In situations where the person is likely to find it hard to feel forgiven by God or to reach the point of forgiving themselves, it may be helpful for the church leaders, on the authority of the word of God, to pronounce cleansing and absolution. They do this as representatives of the church, and it is important that the members of the church who know of the abuse are helped to see that even this sin is forgivable, and that the former abuser should be accepted as any repentant sinner. Sadly, however, the counsellor will almost certainly have to help the person cope with those in the church who choose to treat abuse as some sort of unforgivable sin.

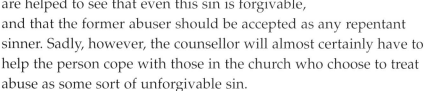

4. **Help the abuser change patterns of thinking and behaviour.** New patterns may arise out of the analysis of the root causes of the abuse. Where a man has, for example, turned to relationships with children because he cannot develop satisfying relationships with adults, help must be given to change the mindset dominated by low self-esteem, and practical steps decided on to develop secure and trusting friendships with adults. Other practical steps will be obvious, for example, in the case of a church youth worker, finding areas of service which do not bring him into contact with children. As in other areas of sexual sin, the power of temptation to fall back into it, often years afterwards, should never be underestimated, and no risks should be taken.

5. **Ensure that others involved receive the counselling and help they need.** This will include family members who knew what was going on and those whose trust has been betrayed. Though, tragically, abuse within the family often destroys that family altogether, there may be some situations where the counsellor will need to help the whole family through the experience of facing the fact of abuse, coming to terms with it, and rebuilding the family out of the ruins. In this situation commitment, determination, the ability to forgive, and the power of the grace of God and the work of the Holy Spirit, are all foundational. Even if other family members are not willing to receive specialized counselling, they may find it useful to join a support group of people who have gone through similar experiences.

Besides having a responsibility to take action if evidence of the existence of abuse is observed in the children who are involved in the church's activities, a local church also needs to:

- Be careful about the way we present teaching like 'Children, obey your parents'.

- Watch for youth workers who are at risk.

- Have as standard a code of behaviour for youth workers, for example a rule never to invite children singly to their homes, and procedures at camps and youth weekends. Such a code not only lessens the risk of abuse happening but it can also protect youth workers against false accusations being made.

- If serious abuse does happen within a church, then the authorities *must* be informed, however great the temptation to hush it up – ideally by the abuser himself (or herself) going to the police and confessing what he has done. This is a very hard step to take, and the counsellor will need to provide consistent support both at this stage and through any subsequent prosecution. Needless to say, willingness to take the initiative in going to the police, co-operation with subsequent enquiries, and willingness to receive counselling, can all help as mitigating factors. In a recent case in which I was slightly involved it made the difference between prison and a suspended sentence.

- The issue of church discipline in this and other sexual areas will be dealt with differently by different churches. Some churches will feel that, once the person has repented and been forgiven, no disciplinary action is required. Others will argue that action is needed, both to underline the seriousness of the sin, and to demonstrate that it is not being condoned in any way. Where action is taken, something like the suspension of membership for a limited period, and then full and complete restoration (allowing for the fact that, say, future involvement in children's work will not be permitted) seems the most helpful course pastorally, and it has some biblical precedent in 1 and 2 Corinthians. If a church should choose to remove a person from church membership altogether, it needs to recognize that it has a pastoral responsibility to ensure not only that they join another church, but that the process of counselling and healing continues.

- As in so many other areas, the local church has here a great opportunity to practise and show to the world a powerful combination of clear standards of right and wrong with a message of hope and healing, implemented with extraordinary grace and love and patience, however difficult and costly that may be, and backed up by the supernatural power of the Holy Spirit to cleanse, restore, and even bring about ultimate good. This is pastoral care and counselling at its best.

STUDY GUIDES

INTRODUCTION

Welcome to this Study Guide, to be used with *People, Problems and God*, as part of the Baptist Union of Great Britain Christian Training Programme.

You will see there are three sections. The first is for those who are working through the manual on their own. For each unit there are several exercises, ranging from 'Tick the right boxes' to developing a case study. These will all be most valuable if you actually put pen to paper. My answers to most of the questions are given in the third section; but pastoral counselling is a subject where answers can't always be given that are clearly right and wrong, so don't worry too much if you disagree with my answer on occasion – provided you can think up a good justification why your answer is better than mine.

The second section gives some material for group study. Any of the material in Section One can also be adapted for group use.

STUDY GUIDE SECTION ONE
FOR INDIVIDUAL STUDY

UNIT 1

A Before you begin the unit

We'll start off with a quiz. It is on the material in the first unit, some of which will probably be familiar to you already. Being multiple choice, it won't take you long to work through; just put a tick in the box that seems to you to give the nearest to correct answer; if you feel that more than one of the alternatives is correct, tick them both, or all. Some questions you'll find easy; some not so easy. When you've finished the unit you may like to have another go at it, using the second set of boxes, and see if your score has improved.

Answers will be in Section 3 of this study guide, as well as in Unit 1. Don't worry if you get a low score; it means your improvement will look spectacular the second time round!

1. Who can do Christian counselling?

    a. Only ministers and church leaders. ☐ ☐
    b. Any Christian who is concerned to help others and has a fair level of sensitivity and common sense. ☐ ☐
    c. Any Christian who has been trained in counselling. ☐ ☐

2. The psychoanalytical approach to counselling …

    a. … seeks to understand present problems in terms of past experiences. ☐ ☐
    b. … seeks to understand behaviour in terms of the inner, often unconscious, person. ☐ ☐
    c. … is only relevant for people suffering from psychosis. ☐ ☐
    d. … stems from the work of Sigmund Freud (1856–1939). ☐ ☐
    e. … depends on the use of drugs and hypnosis for its effectiveness. ☐ ☐

f.   … is now almost totally abandoned by contemporary counsellors.   ☐   ☐

3.   How would you define 'superego'?

   a.   Someone with a domineering personality.   ☐   ☐
   b.   Extreme self-centredness.   ☐   ☐
   c.   The 'higher' part of a person that seeks to monitor the more 'base' desires.   ☐   ☐

4.   What is behaviourism?

   a.   The scientific study of people's external behaviour.   ☐   ☐
   b.   An approach to counselling that stresses the changing of behaviour patterns as opposed to the healing of inner hurts.   ☐   ☐

5.   Some approaches to counselling teach that for the most part we are not responsible for the kind of people we are; others stress our responsibility. Which of the following stress(es) our responsibility?

   a.   Sigmund Freud   ☐   ☐
   b.   B F Skinner   ☐   ☐
   c.   Carl Rogers   ☐   ☐
   d.   Victor Frankl   ☐   ☐

B   PSYCHOANALYSIS, PSYCHODYNAMIC COUNSELLING, BEHAVIOURISM, CARL ROGERS, GESTALT THERAPY, LOGOTHERAPY

As you work through these surveys you might ask these questions of each approach:

- *What are the foundational presuppositions of this approach?*

- *To what extent do they fit in with the biblical understanding of people and their problems?*

- *What aspects of this approach appear incompatible with Christianity?*

- *What useful insights into human behaviour or pastoral care can we get from this approach and incorporate into our own approach to pastoral counselling?*

C This has been a unit full of technical terms. Try writing a brief definition of the following. My answers are in Section 3, as well as in Unit 1 and the Glossary.

1. Gestalt

2. Learned response

3. Catharsis

4. Psyche

5. Regression

6. The id

7. Logotherapy

8. Repression

9. Rogerian counselling

10. Defence mechanism

11. Non-directive

12. Conditioning

13. The unconscious

14. Projection

15. Psychodynamic

D How would *you* seek to help our shy man?

E If you haven't had a second go at the opening quiz yet, here's your chance.

UNIT 2

A As you work through the three Christian approaches to counselling, try asking of each one:

- How relevant and useful is this in seeking to help people with problems?
- How compatible is this approach with basic Christian principles and doctrines?

B At the end of each of the three sections of this unit I've posed some questions, to some extent in criticism of the approaches. Try answering these questions. There won't be any definitive right or wrong answers, but I've had a go at them in the third section, and you may like to check your answers with mine.

C Again, there has been a lot of fairly technical material in this unit, and it wouldn't be too difficult to get the details of the approaches mixed up. To see if you've managed to do this, here are a number of phrases or statements lifted from the unit, each describing the approach of either Lake, Adams or Crabb. Your task is to put L, A or C in the box as you think appropriate. However confused you may be, by the law of averages you ought to get at least 33%!

☐ 1. Spoiling the Egyptians.

☐ 2. The first three months of foetal development.

☐ 3. Every non-organic problem is rooted in relating.

☐ 4. Counselling leads immediately to action.

☐ 5. Sinful living is at the heart of the counselling focus.

☐ 6. Primal pain.

☐ 7. Build up biblical categories, add to them observations from life and reflect on these prayerfully.

☐ 8. Confrontation.

☐ 9. Wrong beliefs lead to wrong goals.

☐ 10. Changed behaviour leads to changed feelings.

☐ 11. Therapeutic alliance.

106

☐ 12. Tangled webs.

☐ 13. Significance and security.

☐ 14. Severe maternal distress.

☐ 15. Problems arise when we seek to be independent of God.

☐ 16. Pastoral counselling is to be done by pastors, not psychiatrists.

☐ 17. God invites us to vent our anger and hurt on him.

☐ 18. Change wrong thinking into right thinking.

☐ 19. Retrace steps to the time and place of the original catastrophe.

☐ 20. Through biblical direction by the Holy Spirit's power Christ enables us to recognise and overcome sinful patterns.

D List four or five ideas you have picked up as you have worked through this unit that you think may be useful in your pastoral counselling.

UNIT 3

A As you work through these principles …

… watch out for elements we touched on in our survey of some Christian counselling approaches in Unit 2.

… think through what these principles have to say about the extent to which we can use the insights of non-Christians into counselling that we were looking at in Unit 1.

B Here's a 'How not to do it' exercise. Judy is on the phone to Ralph. They are both involved in their church's counselling ministry. We can only hear Judy's side of the conversation, but that is enough! It contains several mistakes over issues we've touched on this unit. See if you can find them.

"Yes, I'm fine. The counselling's going all right. An interesting case came to see me yesterday; she's only just started coming to church – sat near old Stan on Sunday – you know who I mean. Well, she swore me to secrecy, and then told me this long tale about a lesbian affair she's been having. Fascinating, it was. Of course I gave it to her straight down the line that she must give it up at once; sent her off to tell the woman she'd never see her again. I've told her she can get back to me if she has any future problems.

Have you had any interesting cases lately?" …

… "Well, it sounds like you get all the good ones. He's certainly a good looking guy; I guess I could probably help him a bit – I've counselled quite a few people with that sort of problem. How about suggesting he comes and sees me?" …

… "Fair enough, I just thought I'd offer. By the way, Gladys had a session with me last week. I knew she'd come in the end, but I've been trying to avoid her. I just can't stand people like her; she's got so many hang-ups it makes me want to scream; I just about did after the first three minutes. She started off; it was all the usual stuff – they're all the same, aren't they? – I let her ramble on for a bit and then broke in and gave her the works. I told her not to come back until she's sorted herself out. I think I might give a piece of my mind to her house group leader; they haven't done anything to sort her out; all they do is 'share' and pray for each other, no deep counselling or anything."

C Here's a 'tick the one that is most nearly right' exercise. If you think there is more than one right answer in a set, tick them both or all.

1. Paraclete means:
   - ☐ a. encourager, helper, supporter, comforter.
   - ☐ b. teacher, instructer, trainer.
   - ☐ c. one who rebukes and corrects.

2. In using the Bible in counselling …
   - ☐ a. … we should always expect Christians and non-Christians to accept its authority.
   - ☐ b. … we should always expect Christians to accept its authority.
   - ☐ c. … we should appeal to its authority to the extent that is acceptable to the person we are counselling.

3. The fact that God is the sovereign creator means, among other things:
   - ☐ a. we can help people to see they are not the product or victims of chance.
   - ☐ b. we have to accept that all our actions are predetermined.
   - ☐ c. we are able to base our counselling on the conviction that God can in the end bring something good even out of the most disastrous situation.

4. Somebody who has come to you for help bursts into tears. Do you:
    ☐ a. leave the room until they've got over it?

    ☐ b. offer them a tissue and tell them to pull themselves together?

    ☐ c. wait quietly?

    ☐ d. assure them that it is OK for them to express their feelings in this way?

5. When someone is talking about their problems:
    ☐ a. listen, and make it clear that you are listening.

    ☐ b. keep a tape recorder running so that you can listen to it again later.

    ☐ c. make it as easy as possible for them to say what they need to say.

    ☐ d. stop them each time you want to make a useful point.

6. The role of the counsellor's supervisor should include:
    ☐ a. keeping fully informed of all the details of each person you are counselling.

    ☐ b. advising in general terms about issues that arise.

    ☐ c. keeping an eye on the counsellor's well being.

7. As Christian counsellors …
    ☐ a. … we should be prepared to pray with Christians or non-Christians if they are happy for us to do so.

    ☐ b. … our task is easy because the Holy Spirit does all the work for us.

    ☐ c. … we have nothing to say to those who are not yet Christians, apart from telling them the gospel.

8. Reasons for establishing a church counselling team include:
    ☐ a. a standard can be set for training and procedure.

    ☐ b. better supervision can be provided.

    ☐ c. those with a specific counselling ministry can be recognised and supported by the church.

    ☐ d. those who are not on the team can be prevented from being involved in counselling.

9. Confrontation …

    ☐ a. … is always inappropriate in Christian counselling.

    ☐ b. … should always be done by a small team, preferably including a minister or elder.

    ☐ c. … should be done in a spirit of humility, love, acceptance and prayer.

10. Someone is telling you about their problem and you are suddenly aware that the Holy Spirit is supernaturally giving you insight into the root cause. Do you:

    ☐ a. interrupt them because now you have got the answer?

    ☐ b. wait till they have finished talking and tell them you have the answer?

    ☐ c. listen carefully as they continue talking and check if the answer you have received fits what they are saying?

    ☐ d. at an appropriate time tentatively introduce 'the answer' and see how they react?

D In the light of this unit, try drawing up your personal 'Ten basic principles for Christian counselling'.

UNIT 4

A Add a few words to complete these statements.

1. The final choice about prayer for healing _

_ _

2. If someone who has just been told they are terminally ill refuses to believe it, we should _

3. We should seek to counter the dehumanizing effect of illness by _ _ _ _ _ _ _ _

_ _

4. When we are with a non-Christian who is dying, we should _ _ _ _ _ _ _ _ _ _ _

_ _

5. If someone is in a coma, remember _

_ _

6. We can help a person look on their time of illness positively by _ _ _ _ _ _ _ _ _ _

   _

7. When praying in general with a person who is ill _ _ _ _ _ _ _ _ _ _ _ _ _ _ _ _

   _ _ _ _ _ '_ _

8. If someone protests they have always been good and so should not be ill _ _ _

   _

9. Anger expressed at doctors or family members by a person who is ill can often be
   understood as _

   _

10. Prayer for healing can follow various patterns, such as _ _ _ _ _ _ _ _ _ _ _ _

    _

B Take a real life experience of serious illness or bereavement that you or someone
you know has been through.

- As far as you can, analyse the feelings, reactions, and processes involved.

- Were there any distinguishable 'stages'?

- What kind of pastoral care (support, counselling, love, 'a shoulder to cry on', and so
  on) were required, and when?

- What comments and attitudes from would-be helpers were unhelpful, and which
  helped most? Why was this so?

C Here's a TRUE/FALSE/IN BETWEEN quiz. If you think the statement is true, give
it a T. If you think it is false, give it an F. If it is half true, or sometimes true, or true in
some qualified way, give it a P (for POSSIBLY, or PERHAPS).

☐ 1. We should discourage people from expressing grief at funerals.

☐ 2. Keeping a room exactly as a dead loved one left it is an indication that the
bereaved person may have got stuck in the earliest stages of the grief
process.

☐ 3. The grieving process rarely lasts longer than a year.

☐ 4. Christians shouldn't grieve when the loved one has gone to be with the Lord.

☐ 5. Who you are and what you do is generally more important in the early days of bereavement than what you say.

☐ 6. The 'farewell to the body' element of a funeral can be very significant.

☐ 7. The practice of making funerals of Christians triumphant affairs should be resisted.

☐ 8. Once a bereaved person shows signs of 'getting over it' they can be left to look after themselves.

☐ 9. It is very wrong for a bereaved Christian to have an experience of feeling that the dead person is in the room with them.

☐ 10. If there has been some problem in the bereaved person or in their relationship with the person who has died, it is more likely there will be problems in the grief process.

UNIT 5

A Have a go at producing a check list of topics that ought to be covered in a series of marriage preparation sessions. Since the list will probably be pretty long, try putting an asterisk by topics which seem essential for all couples, as opposed to issues which may or may not be relevant to a particular couple.

B Spot the intruders! Five of these principles in marriage counselling are 'right' and five are 'wrong'. Spot the ones you think are wrong and write a couple of sentences saying why.

1. As with alcoholics, always wait until couples with marriage problems are desperate before getting involved.

2. Don't bring religion into your counselling if neither of the couple are practising Christians.

3. Where possible, get the individual partner or the couple to prescribe the steps that they should take.

4. 'Marriage enrichment week-ends' are designed for those with problems in their marriages.

5. You are not likely to get far if one of the partners is not interested in saving the marriage.

6. Deal with causes, not just symptoms.

7. It is safe to assume that both partners are well aware of what the problems are.

8. Take feelings seriously.

9. Christian love doesn't love for what it can get out of the other person.

10. Very few Christian couples have problems in their marriages.

C Try writing an imaginary case study about a couple who come to you for help after the husband has been having an affair, or an individual who seeks help over his or her homosexuality. Summarise briefly:

1. the problem.

2. your approach to counselling.

3. what comes out in the initial exploration.

4. the approach to solving the problems.

5. the ups and downs of the healing process.

UNIT 6

A Think of three people in your church who tend to stand out from the crowd; if they have one or two awkward personality traits, so much the better. Then have a go at doing a personality type analysis on each of them. Don't worry about lots of technical terms; concepts like 'caring', 'visionary', 'strong willed', 'sensitive', 'a follower', will do perfectly adequately. Then add into the picture what you know of their background and past.

To what extent does the picture you have drawn help your understanding of how they could find themselves involved in conflict with others in the church?

B Write a few lines on each of these concepts which we've touched on in this unit.

1. Growth through conflict.

2. Mediation.

3. Changing attitudes.

4. Justifying a stance.

5. Saving face.

6. Drawing in allies.

7. "God will never bless this church while X is part of it."

8. "There's no problem as far as I'm concerned."

9. Theological disagreement.

10. Apportioning blame.

C Perhaps you have lived through or been part of a major church conflict, or you are able to have a chat with someone who has. Try analysing the way the conflict developed and how it was resolved. In particular, try and find specific mistakes that were made, and see how they could have been avoided.

D Draw up your own ten principles for preventing conflict in your church.

UNIT 7

A How about another TRUE/FALSE/IN BETWEEN quiz? If you think the statement is true, give it a T. If you think it is false, give it an F. If it is somewhere in between give it a P (for POSSIBLY or PERHAPS).

☐ 1. The Bible teaches the body is evil.

☐ 2. A positive self-image and Christlike humility are incompatible.

☐ 3. The inability to love oneself can lead to the inability to accept love from others.

☐ 4. Anorexia is caused by low self-image.

☐ 5. Those who have been brought up in a secure affirming family are unlikely to have a problem with self acceptance.

☐ 6. In order to stretch children, parents and teachers should always set them goals that are just beyond what they can reach.

☐ 7. Self-doubt and questions like 'Am I normal?' usually stop by the mid-teens.

8. Since the breakdown of secure structures is one of the hallmarks of our society, we should expect that a lot of people will have a problem with self-acceptance.

9. Aggression and criticism of others is caused by low self-image.

10. A person with low self-image will find it difficult to accept God's love, forgiveness, acceptance, and so on.

B Counsellors don't always get it right. Here are Tom's notes from his counselling with Garry, aged 17. Try writing a sentence or two – positive or critical – for each point I've numbered.

12 May. Session with G. Very hard going. He's like a frightened mouse. Didn't do any real probing; just trying to get to know him and put him at his ease. (1)

15 May. Had a chance to spend time with G on the church walk. He seemed to

avoid peer company. We talked about his stamp collection and long solitary cycle rides. He's much too introverted. Told him to get involved in more social activities. (2)

19 May. Good progress with G; really opening up. He's a bag of fears and insecurity. Some of what he said was bizarre; had to keep reassuring him I didn't think he was crazy. (3)

26 May. Difficult session with G. Clammed up again. After half an hour of frustration I told him it wasn't worth wasting our time if he wouldn't talk, and sent him away. (4)

7 July. Been feeling bad about G; he seems worse. Asked him to take me for a cycle ride – I need the exercise. But every time I tried to get onto the real issues he clammed up. (5)

16 July. Good session with G. I tried not pushing him, and he opened up much more readily. (6) A grim background; no known father, rejected by mother, abused by stepfather; bullied while in care. If he hadn't been fostered by a Christian couple he'd be wreck by now. Can't understand why three years of security plus becoming a Christian haven't solved his problems. (7)

23 July. Good progress with G. Got him to describe himself – it was all pretty negative – and trace back where these ideas came from. I kept gently saying things like: "But what your stepfather said about you wasn't necessarily true". Didn't push him; he's got to move at his own pace. (8)

30 July. Tried to get G to list some of his strengths. Not a lot of progress. (9)

6 August. Great session with G. He was prayed for after the communion service; went flat out on the floor, and had an incredible experience of God's love and acceptance. He kept saying "God is my father, and he thinks I'm great". Well, praise the Lord, I can sign him off now; he won't need any more counselling. (10)

C Martin's counselling approach to Sally is similar in many ways to Larry Crabb's *Biblical Counselling*. Outline a few suggestions on how someone following Jay Adams' *Nouthetic Counselling* approach might have counselled Sally.

UNIT 8

A Try writing a few lines on each of these concepts/statements, in the context of child abuse.

1. Don't promise confidentiality.

2. God as father.

3. Ritual abuse.

4. The development of abuse.

5. "If you tell anyone, daddy'll be sent to prison."

6. Possible indications of sexual abuse.

7. Emotional abuse.

8. Malicious allegations of sexual abuse.

9. When the police and social services step in.

10. An abused child's feelings of guilt.

B Here are some statements on the subject of adults who have been sexually abused as children. Some are true, some are false. See if you can spot the false ones and give reasons why they are false.

☐ 1. If suppressed memories of childhood abuse emerge they should be taken seriously.

☐ 2. A person's inability to remember a substantial section of their childhood is a clear indicator of sexual abuse.

☐ 3. During a time of ministry the Holy Spirit may reveal the existence of suppressed childhood abuse.

☐ 4. If a victim feels guilty, they should be helped to come to the Lord in confession and then be given assurance of cleansing.

☐ 5. In any counselling situation we should explore the possibility that childhood abuse is the cause or a contributory factory of the person's problems.

☐ 6. If there is any risk that the abuser is still practising abuse appropriate action must be taken.

☐ 7. The victim must completely forgive the abuser before healing can take place.

☐ 8. The police must be informed about all cases of abuse, however long ago.

☐ 9. Childhood abuse can be a contributory cause of sexual promiscuity.

☐ 10. The psychological and spiritual hold an abuser may have over the victim may be broken by a time of prayer ministry or deliverance.

C What structures/procedures might be put into place in your church to protect children?

STUDY GUIDE SECTION TWO
FOR GROUP STUDY

Any of the material in Section One can be adapted for group use. The quiz type material, for instance, can be used in the group as a whole, or photocopied and done by each individual.

Material from Section One that is particularly suitable for group discussion is included below in a modified form, together with additional group activities. Whatever you do, don't try and cover it all; select what is most appropriate for the group.

Where individuals are invited to introduce a discussion with their personal experience of being counselled, bereavement, or the like, it may be wise to give them a few days' notice so that they can prepare.

UNIT 1

SECULAR APPROACHES TO COUNSELLING

PSYCHOANALYSIS, PSYCHODYNAMIC COUNSELLING, BEHAVIOURISM, CARL ROGERS, GESTALT THERAPY, LOGOTHERAPY

A There is hardly likely to be time in a group situation to analyse all five approaches. If the four questions below are all tackled, it would be wise to concentrate on just one or two of the approaches. Alternatively, one of the questions could be applied to all five approaches.

1. *What are the foundational presuppositions of this approach?*

2. *To what extent do they fit in with the biblical understanding of people and their problems?*

3. *What aspects of this approach appear incompatible with Christianity?*

4. *What useful insights into human behaviour or pastoral care can we get from this approach and incorporate into our own approach to pastoral counselling?*

B Some in the group will have had personal experience of one or more of these counselling approaches. Invite (but don't pressurize) them to give their impressions and reactions.

C Get a volunteer to be the 'shy' man, and let the group loose on him.

UNIT 2

CHRISTIAN APPROACHES TO COUNSELLING

A Again, you will probably need to be selective, but here are two questions the group could discuss about each of the three approaches:

1. *How relevant and useful is this in seeking to help people with problems?*

2. *How compatible is this approach with basic Christian principles and doctrines?*

B Try discussing at least some of the questions I've posed at the end of each of the three sections.

C Again, there will be those in the group who have been helped by Christian counsellors following approaches similar to these three. Invite them to share their experiences and reactions.

D Get individuals to list any specific ideas they have picked up as they have worked through this unit that they think may be useful in their pastoral counselling.

UNIT 3

PRINCIPLES OF CHRISTIAN COUNSELLING

A In twos or threes try role playing a counsellor seeking to help someone who has just been made redundant at fifteen minutes' notice. First time round do it with a non-Christian counsellor counselling someone who happens to be a Christian; then, second time round, assume it is a Christian counsellor helping a Christian. Use your imaginations, and try to highlight the differences between the Christian and non-Christian approaches.

B Invite members of the group each to pick out one or two specifically Christian insights into counselling that they feel are particularly significant. Spend a couple of minutes discussing each of them.

C In the light of this unit, get the group to draw up 'Ten basic principles for Christian counselling'.

UNIT 4

ILLNESS, DEATH AND BEREAVEMENT

A Invite a member of the group who has experienced serious illness or bereavement to talk to the group for ten minutes about the experience, touching on such issues as:

1. The feelings, reactions, and processes involved, and any 'stages' discernible.

2. The pastoral care (support, counselling, love, 'a shoulder to cry on', and so on) that was required or given, and when and how it was given.

3. The comments and attitudes from would-be helpers which were unhelpful, and those that helped most, and why this was so.

B Invite any member of the group who belongs to the medical profession to speak from their angle about the pastoral care of those who are ill.

C Discuss how best the two elements of victory over death and grieving can be kept together in the Christian approach to bereavement; you may in particular like to consider how this can best be done at funeral services.

UNIT 5

MARRIAGE AND SEX

A As a group have a go at producing a check list of topics that ought to be covered in a series of marriage preparation sessions. Since the list will probably be pretty long, try to pick out those topics which seem essential for all couples, as opposed to issues which may or may not be relevant to a particular couple.

B Get the group to plan the contents of the programme for a marriage enrichment week-end for couples in their church.

C Discuss the pros and cons of exercising deliverance ministry for a Christian who has a major sexual problem. How might this be done?

CONFLICT

A Do a simple personality analysis on each person in the group; perhaps the least threatening way of doing this would be to get each person to do the analysis on themselves; alternatively, if the members of the group feel secure enough, the group could analyse each member in turn. Then pick out pairs of relative opposites (extravert/introvert, impulsive/cognitive, visionary/cautious, responsive/self-sufficient, leader/follower, etc), and get them to role play the development of a conflict that is in fact based on differences of personality, but which they treat as a matter of principle. The context could be a deacons' meeting where an issue is raised to which they react in opposite ways.

B Someone in the group will have lived through or been part of a major church conflict. Invite them to talk about the experience, and together try and analyse the way the conflict developed and how it was resolved. In particular, try and find specific mistakes that were made, and see how they could have been avoided.

C Get the group to draw up ten principles for preventing conflict in your church.

LOW SELF-IMAGE

A Use these notes of Tom's counselling with Garry (photocopy them for each person in the group) to get the group to pick out and comment on the good and bad in Tom's counselling.

Counsellors don't always get it right. Here are Tom's notes from his counselling with Garry, aged 17. Try working through it, picking out and commenting on it positively and critically.

12 May. Session with G. Very hard going. He's like a frightened mouse. Didn't do any real probing; just trying to get to know him and put him at his ease.

15 May. Had a chance to spend time with G on the church walk. He seemed to avoid peer company. We talked about his stamp collection and long solitary cycle rides. He's much too introverted. Told him to get involved in more social activities.

19 May. Good progress with G; really opening up. He's a bag of fears and insecurity.

Some of what he said was bizarre; had to keep reassuring him I didn't think he was crazy.

26 May. Difficult session with G. Clammed up again. After half an hour of frustration I told him it wasn't worth wasting our time if he wouldn't talk, and sent him away.

7 July. Been feeling bad about G; he seems worse. Asked him to take me for a cycle ride – I need the exercise. But every time I tried to get onto the real issues he clammed up.

16 July. Good session with G. I tried not pushing him, and he opened up much more readily. A grim background; no known father, rejected by mother, abused by stepfather; bullied while in care. If he hadn't been fostered by a Christian couple he'd be wreck by now. Can't understand why three years of security plus becoming a Christian haven't solved his problems.

23 July. Good progress with G. Got him to describe himself – it was all pretty negative – and trace back where these ideas came from. I kept gently saying things like: "But what your stepfather said about you wasn't necessarily true". Didn't push him; he's got to move at his own pace.

30 July. Tried to get G to list some of his strengths. Not a lot of progress.

6 August. Great session with G. He was prayed for after the communion service; went flat out on the floor, and had an incredible experience of God's love and acceptance. He kept saying "God is my father, and he thinks I'm great". Well, praise the Lord, I can sign him off now; he won't need any more counselling.

B Martin's counselling approach to Sally is similar in many ways to Larry Crabb's 'Biblical Counselling'. Invite members of the group to role play how someone following Jay Adams' 'Nouthetic Counselling' approach might have counselled Sally.

C Stage a debate on the motion: The current emphasis on promoting a positive self-image is unbiblical.

UNIT 8

CHILD ABUSE

A Pick out some of the following issues for discussion in the group:

1. Don't promise confidentiality.

2. God as father.

3. Ritual abuse.

4. The development of abuse.

5. "If you tell anyone, daddy'll be sent to prison."

6. Possible indications of sexual abuse.

7. Emotional abuse.

8. Malicious allegations of sexual abuse.

9. When the police and social services step in.

10. An abused child's feelings of guilt.

B It may be that someone in the group has experienced abuse as a child, and would be willing to talk about issues relevant to counsellors, either for those counselling children, or counselling adults who have been abused as children.

C Get the group to draw up principles, structures and procedures that could be put in place in their church to protect children.

STUDY GUIDE SECTION THREE
RESPONSES TO SECTION ONE

SECULAR APPROACHES TO COUNSELLING

A I expect that first time through you'll have found this pretty difficult. Don't worry; second time through is bound to be better!

Remember, edges tend to be pretty fuzzy in the area of pastoral counselling. You are quite free to question my judgment if we disagree; but, at any rate, here are my answers.

1. b and c are both right, though the level they should counsel at may differ.

2. a, b, and d are all right. Psychoanalysis has certainly been used in cases of psychosis, but on plenty of other problems as well. Drugs and hypnosis are still used by some, but they are not essential for psychoanalysis. And plenty of contemporary counsellors use psychoanalytic insights.

3. c is correct.

4. Both a and b are right. If you said b is wrong on the grounds that it is strictly a definition of behaviourist *therapy*, you get an extra star in your crown.

5. c and d are correct. Rogers and Frankl both stress the responsibility and freedom of the individual.

C 1. Pattern or whole. Gestalt therapy is an approach to understanding and helping people based on concepts of the whole person and wholeness.

2. A Behaviourist term for a pattern of behaviour that we have learnt to follow in response to a given stimulus.

3. The dealing with the destructive power of experience and emotions by bringing them to the surface and expressing and off-loading them, sometimes in dramatic ways.

4. The inner self.

5. A defence mechanism in which the person escapes from the unwelcome present by going back to behaviour appropriate to the past, especially childhood or infancy.

6. The basic instincts and energies at the heart of the human psyche.

7. An approach to counselling stressing personhood and meaning advocated by Victor Frankl.

8. A defence mechanism, pushing unwelcome thoughts and experiences out of the conscious mind and into the unconscious.

9. An affirming and optimistic approach advocated by Carl Rogers based on the belief that we all have within ourselves what is needed to solve our problems.

10. A subconscious device we adopt to cope with the undesirable desires that arise from the id.

11. An approach to counselling in which the counsellor allows the person to control the direction of the conversation.

12. The process of establishing a specific response to a stimulus.

13. The part of the person where past experiences are stored without our awareness of them.

14. A defence mechanism in which a person locates in someone else undesirable elements found in themselves.

15. A term for a variation on psychoanalysis which emphasizes the complex interactions in the person.

UNIT 2

CHRISTIAN APPROACHES TO COUNSELLING

B Here are my comments; necessarily, they tend to reflect my personal assessment of the three approaches. But they may be useful for you to compare with yours.

FRANK LAKE

There is some truth in Lake's basic theory, but surely not the whole truth. Even more than most things in the area of psychology and counselling it could never be finally shown to be true, though there may be ways of demonstrating that it is false.

I tend to feel that a lot of the benefit from this approach arises from the long-term experience of being cared for and listened to.

No. Lots of people have been helped using other types of approach.

I tend to feel it is a secular approach with Christian additions – though that doesn't make it wrong.

No. Otherwise we'd be implying that anyone who has had a good secure life up to adulthood will never have any problems.

It has part of the truth, but not all; though, again, that doesn't necessarily condemn it.

JAY ADAMS

If you define counselling in Adams' narrow sense, his theology fits. But most of us want to have a broader concept of counselling, to include, say, helping a bereaved person.

I don't feel Adams has a fully balanced understanding of the Bible's teaching and examples in the field of counselling.

Some seem to believe that nothing can be achieved without dozens of counselling sessions; others seem to expect instant results. For me it will largely depend on the person and their problems; certainly some will need long term counselling, just as some will need just one or two sessions.

I am sure we can help non-Christians; we can, for instance, show them love and acceptance, and give them encouragement and advice without any reference to Christianity. But I also believe that many non-Christians will be willing to let us bring in our Christian principles while talking with them, and even pray with them.

Yes.

LARRY CRABB

Of course in our counselling theory and theology we should start with God rather than our needs. Crabb would claim that he does so; it is the *application* that starts with us and our needs. But the criticism that it smacks a bit of 'I have a right to be happy' may be a valid one.

This is the kind of situation where we need something stronger than human wisdom or the power of positive thinking, or even getting a biblical mindset. Crabb's approach won't get far without the power of the Holy Spirit.

I think it does; even if the 'right beliefs' are not specifically Christian, they can still be a great improvement on the 'wrong beliefs'.

C

1. C
2. L
3. C
4. A
5. A
6. L
7. C
8. A
9. C
10. A and C
11. L. It is Lake's phrase, though Adams and Crabb would both want to claim the concept; maybe Crabb has a better claim than Adams.
12. C
13. C
14. L
15. C
16. A

17. L

18. C

19. L

20. A. The phrase is Adams'. Crabb would agree with the sentiment.

UNIT 3

PRINCIPLES OF CHRISTIAN COUNSELLING

B Here are the ones I found; some are more serious than others; and you may have picked up one or two I've missed …

1. There are several ways Judy hardly seems to reflect the love and grace of Jesus to those she is trying to help, especially using the word 'case' to refer to a person, and her attitude to Gladys.

2. Confidentiality! ("She swore me to secrecy, and then …")

3. Elements of unwholesome interest, seen in "Fascinating, it was" and the willingness to take on the good-looking guy.

4. Phrases like "I gave it to her straight down the line" and "I gave her the works" don't sound too reassuring.

5. Doubtless there are good grounds for an immediate end to the lesbian relationship. But it is a huge step Judy is asking the woman to take. A lot more preparation for it, and support in it, would seem to be called for. And as for "Come back *if* you have any future problems" …

6. It hardly sounds as if she listened to Gladys in a warm accepting loving atmosphere!

7. No one person is ever the same as anyone else.

8. Listen; very rarely interrupt.

9. Of course Gladys needs deep counselling; but that's not the role of the housegroup. They seem to be doing just what they should do, supporting, praying and loving. The 'deep counselling' is Judy's responsibility, and it looks like she's blown it.

C

1. a

2. c. We may accept its authority, but quite a few Christians, not to mention non-Christians, have problems in this area.

3. a and c. We can believe in predestination without having to accept that every action of our lives (for example whether we have one or two pieces of toast for breakfast) is predetermined.

4. c and d (if necessary). Don't abandon them, and don't make them feel bad about expressing emotion; it will amost certainly help them.

5. a and c. Assume every counselling session is confidential, unless you both agree it isn't. Listen! Never mind the useful points; there may be a time for them later; but don't stop listening.

6. b and c. Details of what goes on in the counselling times should be treated as confidential unless the person gives permission for them to be passed on. There may well be times when you feel a bit out of your depth and will need to ask the person's permission to divulge some details to your supervisor so that you can get the guidance you need.

7. a. Sometimes the Holy Spirit does all the work; but generally we have to do some too!

8. a, b and c. If you ticked d as well, you could get away with it as long as you meant 'more advanced counselling'. We must never try to stop anyone engaging in basic counselling in the form of listening, encouraging, supporting, and so on.

9. c. It is sometimes appropriate. There may be times when it should be done by the 'heavies'; but Matthew 18:15–17 hints that a one to one confrontation should be the first step.

10. c and d.

UNIT 4

ILLNESS, DEATH AND BEREAVEMENT

A Each person will complete the statements in their own words. Here are mine.

1. The final choice about prayer for healing rests with the person who is ill.

2. If someone who has just been told they are terminally ill refuses to believe it, we should accept this as a normal reaction, and allow them some days to come to terms with the news.

3. We should seek to counter the dehumanizing effect of illness by relating normally to them, reassuring them, affirming their value and showing them special love.

4. When we are with a non-Christian who is dying we should resist the temptation to take advantage of them in any way; if they are happy for us to share the gospel or pray with them, we must do it with great sensitivity and gentleness.

5. If someone is in a coma, remember they still may be able to hear you.

6. We can help a person look on their time of illness positively by being sensitively positive ourselves, and encouraging them to accept that God is in control and can bring good out of it.

7. When praying in general with a person who is ill be brief and simple, praying for them and their immediate concerns, possibly holding their hand or putting a hand on their shoulder.

8. If someone protests that they have always been good and so should not be ill, don't start a theological argument with them. When appropriate, sensitively point out that Jesus suffered though he was sinless, and that illness and suffering have always been the common lot of good and bad.

9. Anger expressed at doctors or family members by a person who is ill can often be understood as a projection of the anger felt towards the illness itself.

10. Prayer for healing can follow various patterns such as anointing with oil, laying on of hands, one to one, by the elders, by a prayer ministry team, in the context of a communion service or a 'healing' service or a house group, or in private.

C 1. F. People need to express grief, and the funeral is an appropriate place.

2. T. It can be a sign that the person has not accepted that the person is dead.

3. F. It can last a lifetime. Perhaps the average is two to five years.

4. F. We don't grieve without hope, but we still miss them and are sad. Jesus wept at the grave of Lazarus; grieving is an expression of love.

5. T.

6. T. It can be an important step in accepting that the person has died and that the process of adjusting has to begin.

7. F or P. They should be both triumphant and an opportunity to express grief.

8. F. The grieving process will have lots of ups and downs. Don't abandon the person on the first up.

9. F. It is a fairly common experience, when the mind reverts to what it has experienced for so long. Clearly, we should do what we can to discourage fantasy, and it is certainly wrong for people to try and contact the dead; but the odd experience of this sort isn't anything to worry about.

10. T. It is more likely, but by no means inevitable.

UNIT 5

MARRIAGE AND SEX

A Again, lists will vary. Here's mine. You'll see I've found it hard not to put an asterisk against every item!

*Understanding each other. *Communication. *Concepts of (Christian) marriage. *Roles. *Love/Christian love. *Biblical teaching on marriage, love, relationships, family. *Facing friction, problems and pressures. *Coping with change. *Praying and growing together as Christians. Work. Finance. In-laws. Sexual issues. Children. Recreation and relaxation. Their role in the church. *The marriage service, especially the vows.

B 1 is wrong; get in as soon as you can, before things get too serious.

2 is wrong as a blanket principle. It will be inappropriate in some cases, but in others it will be a good opportunity to introduce some alternative principles for the future. And the chances are they will have been married in church and were reasonably serious about it on the day.

4 is wrong. Their aim is to make good marriages better.

7 is wrong. It may be wisest to assume the opposite! Communication is likely to be poor, and each partner may only be interested in themselves.

10 is wrong. Very few people, Christians or non-Christians, get away with no problems. More openness in this area would make it easier for those with serious problems to admit to them before it is too late.

UNIT 6

CONFLICT

B Points you could have included are:

1. Make growth the goal: growth over the specific issue, personal growth, and growth in understanding of Christian principles and the power of the gospel.

2. A mediator needs to be acceptable to both sides, wise, inspiring trust, able to exercise the right degree of authority and leadership, and, above all, able to bring the grace and power of Christ into the situation.

3. Attitudes are hard to change; it takes time, forbearance and grace. Help people to distinguish between attitudes to issues and to the people involved in the issues. Counter attitudes based on false information or ignorance by true information and personal contact.

4. People in conflict consciously or unconsciously seek to justify the stance they are taking by stressing that it is a major issue, making it a theological matter, finding further faults in the people on the other side, and drawing in allies.

5. Within reason, it is a matter of Christian grace to make it as easy as possible for the people involved to set a resolved conflict behind them. So avoid humiliating anyone, and even express appreciation for raising and resolving the issues in a positive way.

6. Part of justifying a stance. It's a lot less lonely, and it makes your case look stronger.

7. The high point of a process of conflict escalation; it is no longer a matter of deciding an issue; the person opposing you must be destroyed (though, of course, the commitment to destroy is expressed in spiritual language).

8. "It's not me, it's the other person." The counsellor will avoid apportioning blame, but can point out that even if it is right that there is no problem, the other person thinks there is, so something has to be done, if only for the sake of the 'weaker' brother or sister.

9. Should be taken seriously, even if (as is often the case) theology has only been dragged in to bolster a case or make it look spiritual. Points include: accept that each side has valid insights; God is speaking through each for the enrichment of all; find and stress common ground; stress that theological disagreement does not entail separation.

10. Avoid it. Everyone else will be doing it; better for you to risk the mistake of being too generous with praise than with blame.

UNIT 7

LOW SELF-IMAGE

A 1. F or possibly P. A lot of the passages that used to be taken as teaching this are now interpreted as referring to the fallen sinful nature, not the body as such.

2. F. Jesus had both, and he's our example.

3. T.

4. P. Low self-image is a major cause of anorexia, but it wouldn't be fair to say that *all* anorexia is caused by it. If you put F for this reason you are right. Since I'm in a generous mood, if you put T appreciating this point, you are right as well!

5. T or P. They are certainly less likely.

6. F. This isn't the best way to stretch children, and it is likely to deprive them of praise and affirmation and achievement.

7. F. The mid-teens period is often packed with self-doubt, and for lots of people it goes on into adulthood.

8. T.

9. P, F or T on the same (generous) basis as 4.

10. T.

B
1. Good; important to build up a secure relationship as a basis for counselling, especially with frightened mice.

2. Probably a bit early to be telling him to do something that is obviously very hard for him.

3. Good. Garry needs to unload, and it is vital that Tom makes it easy for him to do so openly.

4. Two mistakes. Apart from the bad one of expressing his frustration, Tom should have been aware that this was likely to be a difficult session. Garry has been feeling extra insecure all week as a result of the things he confessed to Tom last time. He is embarrassed that Tom now knows so much about him, and scared that he is going to probe deeper. So he clams up. Tom should have accepted this, and used the session to build up trust, talking about general things.

5. The cycle ride is a good idea – but give the lad space!

6. Tom's getting the point.

7. Tom should understand. Fourteen years of rejection and abuse don't go away easily. Becoming a Christian doesn't solve every problem instantly, though it does open the door to God's healing power.

8. Good.

9. Good policy, though it needs patience.

10. Wow! Tom is right to accept this as a genuine intervention by God; even if he had his doubts about it, it would be very unwise to express those to Garry. But he's quite wrong to sign him off. Even if he doesn't need any more counselling, the last thing Garry wants is to be dropped by Tom. And he is almost certainly going to need more counselling. God's supernatural intervention is part (a very significant part) of the process of healing, not the end of it.

CHILD ABUSE

A The kind of things you could have mentioned include:

1. It may well be necessary to pass the information on.

2. A child who has been betrayed by her/his own father is going to have difficulty with this concept; wise and careful teaching will be needed.

3. Includes ritual sex acts as well as religious rituals. It certainly exists, but convictions are very hard to get.

4. Often, though not always, abuse starts in a small way, and only gradually develops to regular intercourse.

5. Various threats may be used to ensure that a child remains silent.

6. Changes in mood or behaviour, especially withdrawal; inappropriate relationships; unexplained injuries; inappropriate sexual knowledge or talk; persistent tiredness.

7. Shouting, taunting, threats, rejection.

8. These do happen; nevertheless all allegations should be taken very seriously. The fact that some malicious allegations have been made must not be taken as an excuse for inaction or a cover-up.

9. Such action is generally drastic and shattering for a family. A high level of support will be needed for everyone involved.

10. This can arise through the sense of defilement or because the child enjoyed or encouraged the abuse in some way, or because their telling has broken up the family. She or he may need help with this through confession and the assurance of God's forgiveness. Prayer for cleansing from guilt may be appropriate even when you are convinced the child is fully innocent.

B
1. T. Take them seriously, but don't assume that they necessarily indicate abuse has taken place.

2. F. It could indicate all sorts of things, not necessarily abuse.

3. T. But be wise in how you handle the 'revelation'.

4. T.

5. F. There are all sorts of counselling situations where it is quite inappropriate. Don't go raking around unless you have good reason to suspect something.

6. T.

7. F. If 'completely' means once and for all, such that they never again feel any anger or resentment, many victims will never reach that point. God doesn't wait till we've reached perfection to heal us; a stated willingness to let God deal with the anger etc is enough to start with. "Lord, I forgive; help my unforgiveness."

8. F. The authorities must be informed if there is a risk of further abuse occurring. There seems little reason to tell the police if the abuser is dead or in a nursing home, and if the victim wishes to take no action.

9. T. It *can* be.

10. T.

APPENDIX A
FURTHER READING

For Units 1 and 2 the most comprehensive introductory survey of secular and Christian approaches to counselling is:

R Hurding *Roots and Shoots*: *a guide to counselling and psychotherapy* Hodder and Stoughton 1986

For Unit 3, the same author has written:

R Hurding *The Bible and Counselling* Hodder and Stoughton 1992

There are many books on general counselling which cover the topics dealt with in Units 4–8. A useful one is:

G Collins *Christian Counselling*: *a comprehensive guide* Word 1985

For specific units a browse through a Christian bookshop will provide plenty of possibilities, written at varying levels. If you are beginning in counselling the following may be particularly useful.

For Unit 4:

H Alexander *Bereavement*: *a shared experience* Lion 1993

For Unit 5:

L Crabb *Men and Women*: *the giving of the self* Marshall Pickering 1991

The two books mentioned in Unit 5 are:

D and J Ames *Looking up the Aisle* Mission to Marriage 1989
J and J Houghton *A Touch of Love* Kingsway 1986

For Unit 6:

J Huggett *Conflict: Friend or Foe?* Kingsway

For Unit 7:

R McGee *The Search for Significance* Word

For Unit 8:

D Allender *The Wounded Heart* CWR

The Baptist Union has produced an excellent booklet on child protection for churches:

A Dunkley (ed) *Safe to Grow* Baptist Union of Great Britain 1994

APPENDIX B
FURTHER STUDY

Many adult education centres, colleges, and independent organisations offer courses in counselling. The British Association for Counselling keeps a register of many of them. To find specifically Christian courses in your area consult the lists provided by the UK Christian Handbook and The Association of Christian Counsellors or enquire from, for example, your local Churches Together grouping.

To pick out just a few: Body House (West Ham Central Mission) offers a range of short evening/Saturday courses in basic counselling. Spurgeon's College offers nationally accredited certificate/diploma courses in counselling through evening and day classes. St John's College offers correspondence courses, one of them validated by the University of Nottingham. Waverley Christian Training Centre (CWR) offer a wide range of courses, from one day through to three weeks residential or a year nonresidential. The Clinical Theology Association holds seminars and courses all over the country.

The Association of Christian Counsellors, 173a Wokingham Road, Reading, Berks RG6 1LT, Tel 01734 662207

Bodey House, Stock Road, Stock, Ingatestone, Essex CM4 9DH, Tel 01277 840668

The British Association for Counselling, 1 Regent Place, Rugby, Warwicks CV21 2PJ, Tel 01788 578328

The Clinical Theology Association, St Mary's House, Church Westcote, Oxford OX7 6SF, Tel 01993 830209

St John's Extension Studies, Bramcote, Nottingham NG9 3DS, Tel 0115-925 1117

Spurgeon's College, 189 South Norwood Hill, London SE25 6DJ, Tel 0181-653 0850

Notes

Notes

Notes

Notes

Notes

Notes